A
DIALO

concerning Witches
and *Witchcraftes.*

In which is laide open how craftely
the Diuell deceiueth not onely the Witches
but many other and fo leadeth them
awrie into many great
errours.

By George Giffard Minifter of Gods
word in Maldon.

LONDON.

Printed by *Iohn Windet* for Tobie Cooke and Mi-
hil Hart, and are to be fold in Pauls Chnrch-
yard, at the Tygers head. 1 5 9 3.

Made and Printed by the Replika Process in Great Britain by
Percy Lund, Humphries & Co. Ltd.
3 Amen Corner, London, E.C.4
and at Bradford

TO THE RIGHT VVOR-
SHIPFVLL MAISTER RO-
bert Clarke, one of her Maiesties Barons
of her Highnes Court of Efchequer.

 Ertaine yeares now paſt, right
Worſhipfull, I publiſhed a
ſmall Treatiſe concerning
Witches, to lay open ſome
of Sathans ſleightes, and ſubtill practiſes, leaſt the ignoran-
ter ſort ſhould be carried a-
wry and ſeduced more and more by them. The
errors be farre more groſſe, and the ſinnes much
greater, into which by meanes of Witches he ſedu-
ceth multitudes, then in common opinion they be
eſteemed. It falleth out in many places euen of a
ſuddaine, as it ſeemeth to me, and no doubt by the
heauy iudgement of God, that the Diuels as it were
let looſe, doe more preuail, then euer I haue heard
of. For when as men haue ſet ſo light by the hea-

A 2   ring

ring of Gods voice to be inſtructed by him, they are iuſtly giuen ouer to be taught by the Diuels, and to learne their waies. Sathan is now hearde ſpeake, and beleeued. He ſpeaketh by coniurors, by ſorcerers, and by witches, and his word is taken. He deuiſeth a number of thinges to be done, and they are put in practiſe and followed. The high prouidence of God Almighty and ſoueraigne rule ouer all, is ſet forth ſo vnto vs in the Scriptures, as that without him a Sparrow can not fall vpon the ground. All the haires of our head are numbred. The Deuils would hurt and deſtroy with bodily harmes, both men and beaſtes and other creatures: but all the Diuels in Hell are ſo chained vp and brideled by this high prouidence that they can not plucke the wing from one poore little Wrenne, without ſpeciall leaue giuen them from the ruler of the whole earth. And yet the Witches are made beleeue that at their requeſt, and to pleaſure them by fulfilling their wrath, their ſpirites doe lame and kill both men and beaſtes. And then to ſpread this opinion among the people, theſe ſubtill ſpirites bewray them, and will haue them openly confeſſe that they haue done ſuch great things, which all the Diuels at any mans requeſt cold neuer doe. For if they could, they would not ſtay to be intreated. God giueth him power ſometimes to afflict both men and beaſtes with bodily harmes : If he can, he

will

will doe it, as intreated and sent by Witches, but for vs to imagin either that their sending doth giue him power, or that he would not doe that which God hath giuen him leaue to doe, vnlesse they should request and send him, is most absurd. There be many diseases in the bodies of men and beastes which he seeth will breake forth vnto lamenes or vnto death, he beareth the witches in hand he doth them : He worketh by his other sort of Witches, whome the people call cunning men and wise women to confirme all his matters, and by them teacheth many remedies, that so he may be sought vnto and honored as God. These things taking root in the hearts of the people, and so making them afraide of Witches, and raising vp suspitions and rumors of sundry innocent persons, many giltles are vppon mens othes condemned to death, and much innocent bloud is shed. How subtilly he continueth these matters, I haue to my smal skill laide open in this slender Treatise. I haue done it in waye of a Dialogue, to make the fitter for the capacity of the simpler sort. I am bolde to offer it vnto your Worship, not vnto one as needeth to be taught in these thinges, being zealously affected to the Gospell, & so grounded in the faith of the high prouidence, that I haue been delighted to heare and see the wise and godly course vsed vppon the seat of Iustice by your Worship, when such haue beene arraigned. I

A 3   offer.

The Epiſtle.

offer it therefore as a teſtimony of a thankeful mind
for fauours and kindneſſe ſhewed towardes me:
and ſo intreat your Worſhippe to accept of it. If
it may doe good vnto any of the weaker ſort
in knowledge I ſhall be glad. If I erre
in any thing being ſhewed it, I will
be ready to correct it.

Your Worſhips in all dueties
to commaund.

George Giffard.

Samuell. Daniell. The wife of Samuell. M. B.
Schoolemaiſter. The good wife R.

Sam.

ȝou are well mette olde acquaintance, J am glad to
ſée you looke ſo well, howe
doe all our good friendes
in your Countrey.

Dan.

J truſt they be all in
good health, they were
when J came from home,
J am ſorry to ſée you looke
ſo pale, what haue you béene ſicke lately?

Sam. Truely no, J thanke God J haue had my health
pretily well, but yet me thinke my meate doth me no good
of late.

Dan. What is the matter man, doe you take thought
and care for the world : take héede of that, for the Scripture ſaith, worldly ſorrow worketh death. 2. Cor. 7. 10.
Jt is a great ſinne riſing from vnbeléefe, and diſtruſt in
Gods prouidence, when men be ouer penſiue for the world.

Sam. In déede my minde is troubled, but not for that
which you ſay, for J hope in God J ſhall not want ſo long
as J liue.

Dan. Is it any trouble of conſcience for ſinne : Jf it
be, that may turne to good.

Sam. O, no, no. J know no cauſe why.

Dan. Why, what is it then, if J may be ſo bold, J pray
you

you tell me. I thinke you take me for your friend.

Sam. In deede I haue alwaies found you my very good friend, and I am sure you will giue me the best counsell you can, truely we dwell here in a bad countrey, I think euen one of the worst in England.

Dan. Is it so? I thinke you dwell in a fine countrey, in a sweete wholesome aire and fruitfull grounds.

Sam. Aire man? I finde no fault with the aire, there be naughty people.

Dan. Naughty people? where shall a man dwell, and not finde them? swearers, liars, raylers, slaunderers, drunckards, adulterers, riotous, vnthriftes, dicers, and proude high minded persons, are euery where to be founde in great plenty.

Sam. Nay, I doe not meane them, I care not for them. These witches, these euill fauoured old witches doe trouble me.

Dan. What doe you take your selfe to be bewitched?

Sam. No, no, I trust no euill spirite can hurt me, but I heare of much harme done by them: they lame men and kill their cattle, yea they destroy both men and children. They say there is scarce any towne or village in all this shire, but there is one or two witches at the least in it. In good sooth, I may tell it to you as to my friend, when I goe but into my closes, I am afraide, for I see nowe and then a Hare; which my conscience giueth me is a witch, or some witches spirite, shee stareth so vppon me. And sometime I see an vgly weasell runne through my yard, and there is a foule great catte sometimes in my Barne, which I haue no liking vnto.

Dan. You neuer had no hurt done yet, had you by any witch?

Sam. Trust me I cannot tell, but I feare me I haue, for

for there be two or three in our towne which I like not, but
especially an old woman, I haue béene as careful to please
her as euer I was to please mine own mother, and to giue
her euer anon one thing or other, and yet me thinkes shee
frownes at me now and then. And I had a hogge which
eate his meate with his fellowes and was very well to our
thinking ouer night, and in the morning he was starke
dead. My wife hath had fiue or sire hennes euen of late
dead. Some of my neighbours wishe me to burne some
thing aliue, as a henne or a hogge. Others will me in time
to séeke helpe at the handes of some cunning man, before
I haue any further harme. I wold be glad to do for the best.

Dan. Haue you any cunning man hereabout, that doth
helpe?

Sam. There is one, they say, here a twenty miles of at
T. B. which hath holpe many. And thus much I know,
there was one of mine acquaintance but two miles hence,
which had great losses, he lost two or thrée kine, sir hogs,
he would not haue tooke fifteene shillings a hog for them,
and a mare. He went to that same man, and told him hée
suspected an old woman in the parish. And I think he told
me, that he shewed him her in a Glasse, and tolde him shee
had thrée or foure imps, some call them puckrels, one like
a gray catte, an other like a weasell, an other like a mouse,
a vengeance take them, it is great pitty the countrey is
not ridde of them, and told him also what he shoulde doe,
it is halfe a yeare agoe, and he neuer had any hurt since.
There is also a woman at R. H. fiue and twenty miles
hence, that hath a great name, and great resort there is
dayly vnto her. A neighbour of mine had his childe taken
lame, a girle of ten yeares olde, and such a paine in her
backe, that shée could not sit vpright. He went to that
woman, she tolde him he had some badde neighbour, the
childe was forespoken, as he suspected; marry if he would
goe home, and bring her som of the clothes which the child

lay in all night, shee would tell him certainely. He went home, and put a table Napkin about her necke all night, and in the morning tooke it with him, and shee told him the girle was bewitched in deede, and so told him what hee should doe, and he had remedy, the girle is as wel at this day, and a pretty quicke girle. There was another of my neighbours had his wife much troubled, and he went to her, and shee tolde him, his wife was haunted with a Fairy. I cannot tell what shee bad him doe, but the woman is merry at this howre. I haue heard, I dare not say it is so, that shee weareth about her Sainct Iohns Gospel, or some part of it.

Dan. If you haue such cunning men and women, what neede you be so much afraide?

Sam. Alas man, I could teeme it to goe, and some counsell me to goe to the man at T. B. and some to the woman at R. H. And betweene them both I haue lingred the time, and feare I may be spoiled before I get remedy. Some wishe me to beate and claw the witch vntill I fetch bloud on her, and to threaten her that I will haue her hanged, if I knew which were the best I would doe it.

Dan. I perceiue your danger is betweene two stooles.

Sam. It is very true, if I had heard but of one, I should haue gone ere this time, and I am glad that I met with you. I pray you let me haue your best counsell; I trust you beare me good will.

Dan. Truely I will giue you the best counsell I can, which I am sure shall doe you good, if you will followe it, for in deede I pitty your case, it is most certaine you are bewitched.

Sam. Bewitched, doe you thinke I am bewitched? I feele no harme in my body, you make me more afraide.

Dam. Nay I doe not thinke that the olde woman hath bewitched you, or that your body is bewitched, but the diuell hath bewitched your minde, with blindnes and vnbeleefe,

leefe, to draw you from God, euen to worship himselfe , by
seeking help at the hands of deuils. It is a lamentable case
to see how the deuill hath bewitched thousands at this day
to run after him: and euen to offer sacrifice vnto him.

Sam. I defie the deuill, worship him? fie vpon him, I
hate him with all my hart. Do you thinke any seeke help at
his hands? we seek help against him. I think he neuer doth
good, he hurteth, but he neuer helpeth any.

Dan. It is not in these matters to be taken as wee i-
magine, but as the word of God teacheth. What though
a man think he worshippeth not deuils, nor seeketh not help
at their handes, as he is persuaded, nor hath any such in-
tent, is he euer the neere, when as yet it shall be found by
Gods word, that he doth worship them, and seek vnto them
for help?

Sam. Doe you thinke then that there be no witches?
Doth not God suffer wicked people to do harme? Or doe
you thinke that the cunning men doe helpe by the deuill? I
would be glad to reason with you, but I haue smal knowledge in the scripturs. We haue a Schoolemaister that is
a good pretie scholler, they say, in the Latine tongue, one
M. B. he is gone to my house euen now, I pray you let me
intreat you to go thither, you two may reason the matter,
for you are learned.

Dan. I could be content, but it will aske some time,
and I am going to such a place vpon speciall busines.

Sam. I pray you let mee intreat you : Foure or fiue
houres is not so much.

Dan. Well, I will goe with you.

Sam. Wife, I haue brought an olde friend of mine , I
pray thee bio him welcome.

The wife. He is verie welcome. But trulie man, I
am angrie with you, and halfe out of patience, that you go
not to seeke helpe against yonder same olde beast I haue a-
nother hen dead this night. Other men can seeke remedy.

Here is M. B. tels me , that the good wife R. all the laste
weeke could not make her butter come. She neuer rested
vntil she had got her husbande out to the woman at R. H.
and when he came home , they did but heat a spit red hotte,
and thrust into the creame , vsing certaine wordes , as shee
willed him,and it came as kindly as anie butter that euer
she made. I met the olde filth this morning Lord, how sow-
erlie she looked vpon me, & mumbled as she went, I heard
part of her wordes. Ah (quod she) you haue an honest man
to your husband, I heare how he doth vse me. In trueth,
husband,my stomacke did so rise against her,that I coulde
haue found in my heart to haue flowen vpon her,and scratched her,but that I feared she would be too strong for me.
It is a lustie olde queane. I wished that the good wife R.
had bene with me. I pray you , good husbande, let me intreat you to goe to that same good woman , you may ride
thither in halfe a day.

Sam. Wife, I pray thee be content , I haue intreated
this mine olde friend to reason with M. B. for he tels mee
that we be in a verie foule errour.

M. B. I suppose, so farre as my learning and capacitie doe extend,that small reasoning may serue. The worde
of God doeth shew plainlie that there be witches , & commaundeth they should be put to death. Experience hath
taught too too manie, what harmes they doe.   And if anie
haue the gift to minister help against them, shall we refuse
it? Shall we not drinke when we are a thirst ? Shall wee
not warme vs when wee are a colde : It is pitie that anie
man should open his mouth anie way to defend them,their
impietie is so great.

.Dan. For my part,I go not about to defend witches.
I denie not but that the deuill worketh by them. And that
they ought to be put to death. We ought also to seeke remedie against them : but as I told my friend,the deuil doth
bewitch men by meanes of these witches , and lead them
from

from God, euen to follow himself, to offer sacrifice vnto him to worship him, to obey his wil, to commit manie grieuous sinnes, and to be drowned in manifold errours.

M. B. If you haue this meaning, that witches and sorcerers ar bewitched by the deuil, that they forsake God, and follow him, that they worship and obey him, and doe sacrifice vnto him, and commit manie hainous sinnes, I agrée with you, for I tak it, they euen vow themselues to the deuill, or els he would not be so readie to doe them seruice. But if you mean, that such as seek remedie against them, & wold haue them rooted out, be so seduced and mis-led by the deuill, as you speake, I say your speach is rash and foolish, for they that be earnest against witches, be earnest against the deuil, they defie the deuil, they seek to resist him, and to roote out his instruments. Now, if you were a man that had any learning, you should sée, that contraries cannot be in the same subiect, at one instant, in the same part, and in the same respect: how then can a man hate the deuill, defie the deuill and his workes, and yet follow him at one time?

Dan. I know that witches and coniurers are seduced and become the vassals of Satan: they be his seruants, and not he theirs, as you speake. But I mean indeed that multitudes are seduced and led from God, to follow the deuil, by means of witches & coniurers: yea, I speak it of those, not which are caried of a godlie zeale, but of a blinde rage and mad furie against them. If I speake this rashlie and foolishlie, as you say, and your self learned as you boast, and I vnlearned, I shall be the more easilie ouerthrowne. But I speake so truly, and can so well iustifie all that I haue said by the word of God, that your learning and best skill, shall not be able to disproue the same. Your logicke at the first doth faile you. Not that contraries can be in the same subiect at the same instant, in the same part, and in the same respect. But herein you are vtterly blinde and deceiued, that you name contraries, and take it that the first of

them.

them, as namelie, to hate the deuill, to defie him and his
workes, are in them, when as indeed they are in them but
in imagination. For if men say and think they defie the de=
uill and his workes, and through blindnes and infivelitie,
are euen bewitched, and seduced to followe the deuill, and
to do his will, doth their speach and blinde imagination
make the things indeed to be in them? What if a poore beg=
ger woman say and thinke that she is a Queene: is she ther=
fore no begger, begging still her bread? or is she rid of her
lice?

M. B. Nay, if you iudge, I haue done. If men be ear=
nest against the deuill, and defie him and all his workes,
are you to iudge of their conscience, and to say they defie
him but in imagination, and follow him, and worship him
in deede? is not God alone the iudge ouer mens hearts?
Againe, do you compare those that are in their right mind,
with such as be mad, or out of their wits?

Dan. I knowe that God alone is the searcher of the
heart, touching the thinges which lie hid in secrete: But
where things are open and manifest, the tree is known by
the fruits, so far as we may goe. As if a man professe the
faith of Iesus Christ soundlie, in all pointes according to
the word of God, and doth frame his life thereafter in do=
ing good workes: it is verie wicked for anie man to iudge
of him, that he is an hypocrite, and that he doth all of vaine
glorie. And yet it may be that the Lord, who discerneth the
secrete intents of the heart, seeth indeed that he is but an
hypocrite. On the contrarie parte, where a man professeth
in wordes that he doeth defie the deuill and all his workes,
and yet when it commeth to the triall of Gods word, hee is
found to be seduced, and wrapped in blinde errours of the
deuill, in infivelitie, and euill works, in which he fulfilleth
the will of Satan, and honoureth him in the place of God:
Shal we say that this is a good man because of his words
and imagination, that he defieth the deuill and his works?

Wo

Wo be to them that cal good euil, and euil good. Esa. 5.
We may say they are in bad case, except they repent, and
turne from following Satan. But yet I say, that a faithful
man may erre in some of these thinges through weaknesse
of faith, and through ignorance. And therefore, here men
may not be too rash in iudgment. And now wheras you find
fault, that I make comparison between such as be mad and
those that be in their right mind, it is your ignorãce, which
do not consider that ther be two kinds of madnes, or being
out of their right mind, the one for matters of this worlde,
the other for thinges spirituall and heauenlie. There bee
which are in their wittes for this worlde, which touching
spirituall things are as farre awrie in their imaginations,
as the poore beggar, which thinketh she is a goodlie queene.
Doth not the holie Apostle say, that because men receiue
not the loue of the truth, God wil send them strong de-
lusion to beleeue lies. 2. Thess. 2. And what is that, but
that Satan shall seduce, illude and bewitch their minds, to
make them beleeue that they worshippe and follow God,
when they worship and follow him?

M. B, Doe you take that to be S. Paules meaning?
Doth Satan bewitch mens mindes, and leade them into
falsehooode and errour, making them beleeue they worshipp
God, when they worship deuils?

Dan. S. Paul speaketh there indeed of the comming
of the great Antichrist in the power of the Deuill. Nowe,
those which are seduced and worship Antichrist, think they
worship God: but marke what S. John sayth, All the
world wondred, and followed the beast, and worshipped the dragon which gaue power to the beast: & they
worshipped the beast. Reuelat. 13. And looke in the 12.
chapter of the Reuelation, and you shall find that the Dragon, which the Popery doth worship in stead of God, is the
Deuill.

M. B. Trulie I like your wordes well, I am persua-

B 4   ded

ded the deuill doth seduce and bewitch mens mindes: But touching these that seek help at the hands of cunning men and women against witches, I cannot thinke so hardlie of them. I may be awry, I sée well: I will not be obstinate, if the word of God shew me mine errour. Let vs euen friend-ly conferre of the matter. Be not offended with me, and for my part, I will speake all that I knowe or thinke.

Dan. I must intreate you likewise to beare with my plaine speaches. And let vs in the matters procéde from one point to another, standing onlie vpon that, wherein we shall be found to differ in iudgment. And let Gods word be the Iudge betweene vs.

Sam. I like this wel, though I can say but litle, I wil sit and heare you.

Dan. What is the first question that we shal handle?

M. B. I heard you say, if I did not mistake your speach that there be witches that worke by the deuill. But yet I pray you tell me, doe you think there be such? I know some are of opinion there be none.

Dan. It is so euident by the Scriptures, and in all ex-perience, that there be witches which worke by the deuill, or rather I may say, the deuill worketh by them, that such as go about to proue the contrarie, doe shewe themselues but cauillers.

M. B. I am glad we agrée in that point, I hope we shall in the rest. What say you to this ? that the witches haue their spirits, some hath one, some hath more, as two, thrée, foure, or fiue, some in one likenesse, and some in another, as like cattes, weasils, toads, or mise, whome they nourish with milke, or with a chicken, or by letting them sucke now and then a drop of blood: whome they call when they be of-fended with anie, and send them to hurt them in their bo-dies; yea, to kill them, and to kill their cattell?

Dan. Here is great deceit, and great illusion, here the deuil leadeth the ignorant people into foule errours,

by

by which hee draweth them hedlong into manie grieuous
sinnes.

M. B. Nay then I ſee you are awrie, if you denie theſe
things, and ſay they be but illuſions. They haue bene proued, and proued againe, euen by the manifold confeſſions
of the witches themſelues. I am out of all doubt in theſe,
and could in manie particulars lay open what hath fallen
out. I did dwell in a village within theſe fiue yeares, where
there was a man of good wealth, and ſuddainlie within ten
daies ſpace, he had three kine died, his gelding worth ten
pounds fell lame, he was himſelf taken with a gret pain in
his back, & a child of ſeuē years old died. He ſent to the woman at R. H. and ſhe ſaid he was plagued by a witch, ad-
ding moreouer, that there were three women witches in
that towne, and one man witch: willing him to look whom
he moſt ſuſpected: he ſuſpected one old woman, and cauſed
her to be caried before a Iuſtice of Peace and examined:
with much a doe at the laſt ſhee confeſſed all: Which was
this in effect: that ſhe had three ſpirits: one like a cat, which
ſhe called Lightfoot, another like a Toad, which ſhe called
Lunch, the third like a Weaſill, which ſhe called Make-
ſhift. This Lightfoot, ſhe ſaid, one mother Barlie of W.
ſolde her aboue ſixteene yeares agoe, for an ouen cake, and
told her the Cat would doe hergood ſeruice, if ſhe woulde,
ſhe might ſend her of her errand: this Cat was with her
but a while, but the Weaſill and the Toad came and offered
their ſeruice: The Cat would kill kine, the Weaſil would
kill horſes, the Toade would plague men in their bodies.
She ſent them all three (as ſhe confeſſed) againſt this man:
She was committed to the priſon, and there ſhee died before the Aſſiſes. I could tell you of manie ſuch: I had no
minde to dwell in that place any longer.

Dan. You miſtake me, I do not meane that the things
are not, but my meaning is, that the deuill by ſuch thinges
doth beguyle and ſeduce ignorant men, and lead them into

C errours

errours and grieuous sinnes : And let vs examine euerie
parcell of that which you set down in your speach,and you
shall sée no lesse.

M. B. That is it which I would faine sée: You confesse
they haue spirits, some one, some moje, and in such like-
nesses: what errour be the people led into by that?

Dan. First,consider this that ther be multituds & armies
of deuils,as we sée in the gospel, y manie deuils wer entred
into one man,& Christ saying, What is thy name: answer
is made, Legion, for we are manie. Mark. 5. Now, although the deuils be manie,yet they be all caried with such
hatred against God,with such desire to haue him dishono-
red and blasphemed, and burne with such bloudy malice
and crueltie against men,that they bend their studie all together,one helping and furthering another what they can
in their worke: in so much that the Scripture doeth speake
of them,as if they were but one deuill : for S. Peter sayth,
Your aduersarie the deuill goeth about like a roring lion seeking whom he may deuour. 1. Pet.5. And in the
Reuelation chapter 12. all the deuils make that great red
dragon: And our Sauiour doth shewe how close they ioyne
in one,when he saith, If Satan be deuided against Satan,
or if Satan cast foorth Satan,how shall his kingdom endure Matth.12. now then,whether the witch deale, as shé
supposeth,with one spirit,or with manie,it commeth all to
one effect,thus farre, that one dealeth not alone , but with
the helpe of others. So that he or she that hath familiaritie
with one deuill,it is as much as if it wer with an hundreth.
Moreouer,the deuils be spirits, they haue no bodily shape
or likenesse but yet can make an apparance of a shape, as
appeareth by the inchanters before Pharao , when their
rods were turned into serpents in shew. Exod.7. And then
one deuill can séem to be foure or fiue, and foure or fiue can
séeme to be one: It is therefore but the craft of Satan, to
make shewe of moje or lesse.

Doe

M. B. Do you not thinke then, that where the moe deuils be, there is the greater power of Satan?

Dan. Yes, but it can not be discerned be his appearing to the witch in shew of moe oe lesse: For one can seeme ten vnto her, and ten can seeme one.

M. B. Well, I doe not mislike al this, I pray you proceed toward.

Dan. Then further marke well howe the holie Scriptures doe paint out the deuils to bee mightie terrible spirits, full of power, rage, and crueltie, compared to a great fierie red dragon, Reuel. 12. to a greedie oe hungrie lion, that roeeth after the pray, 1. Pet. 5. And called by S. Paul Principalities, and Powers, the Rulers of the darknesse of this world: now, when they take vpon them the shapes of such paltrie vermine, as Cats, Mise, Toads, and Weasils, it is euen of subtiltie to couer and hide his mightie tyrannie, and power which he exerciseth ouer the heartes of the wicked. It is most necessarie foe vs all to know, what strong aduersaries we haue to encounter withall, that we may fly vnto the Lord God, and seek to bee armed with his power against them.

M. B. Well, what will you inferre vpon this? I cannot deny but that the scriptures doe paint out the deuils to be mightie terrible spirits, and so they may be, although they appeare but like Cats oe weasils.

Dan. I doe not say they be not mightie and terrible because they appeare in such shapes, but I affirme, that their appearing so, is to couer and hide their mightinesse and effectuall working, which they exercise in the darke harts of men. And marke well I pray you, the power of deuils is in the hearts of men, as to harden the heart, to blinde the eies of the mind, and from the lustes and concupiscences which are in them, to inflame them vnto wrath, malice, enuy, and cruell murthers: to puffe them vp in pride, arrogancy and vaine glory: to entice them vnto wantonnesse,

and

and whoredomes, and all vncleannesse. And about these
things they worke continually, and with such efficacy, that
without the power of the glorious passion and resurrection of our Lord Iesus Christ, which we haue by faith, they
cannot be withstood, and they will seeme to be but meane
fellowes, busied about making drink that it shall not work
in the fat, in keeping cheese from running, and butter from
comming, in killing hennes or hogges, or making men
lame.

M. B. May they not doe both the one and the other?

Dan. Yea, but this is my meaning, that while they be
occupied about the greatest things, as in stirring vp Ty-
rants and wicked men to persecute, to reproch and blaspheme the Gospell, which pulleth them downe, to set diui-
sion and warres between kingdoms and kings, hatred and
discord between man and wife, and contention betweene
brethren: yea, to set all in a brople and confusion: they would
seeme to be busied about trifles, and about these they busie
mens mindes, that they may not obserue and take heed of
them in those other.

M. B. I perceiue your meaning, but yet I doe not
conceiue whereunto you chiefly tend: for do not they which
looke vpon these harmes done by witches, confesse that the
deuill doth all those things which you mention?

Dan. The ignorant sort, which are so terrified by witches, do in words after a sort, confesse so much as you say,
but when it commeth to the matter, they deny it in effect.
For mark this, the deuils continuallie compasse the soule
of man about, to shoot it full of their fierie dartes. Ephes. 6.
euen to wound it to death with all wicked sinnes. The deuill goeth about like a roring lion, seeking whome hee
may deuour. 1. Pet. 5. And they by this craft which they
vse by means of the witches, make the blind people imagin
that they neuer come nigh them, but when the witches are
angrie and doe send them, and that they are easilie driuen
away

away when they do come, as by burning some quick thing, as henne, or hogge, or by beating and drawing bloud vpon the witch. Such people as can thus driue him away, or by thrusting a spitte red hot into their creame, are farre from knowing the spirituall battel, in which we are to warre vnder the banner of Christ against the deuill, much lesse doe they know how to put on (as S. Paule willeth) the whole armour of God, to resist and ouercome him. Epheſ. 6. He may deale with their soules euen as he listeth, when they take him not present but vpon such sending, and where such hurt doth follow in their bodies or goods.

M. B. I doe not denie, but that the deuils seeke chiefly for to destroy the soules of men: But (as I tak it) you confeſſe, that they being sent by the witches, doe also those bodilie harmes: and as yet I see no reason why they may not seeke remedie against such harmes, and driue him away by anie good meanes: doth the worde of God forbid vs to vse meanes? If I be sicke, shall I not take physicke? If I bee thirstie, shall I not drinke? Indeed I am of your minde, though I did neuer marke so much before, that the deuill dealeth subtillie in this, that by dealing in such small matters, he couereth himselfe in the greater, as though he came not neere, nor did not medle but in such maner: But here standeth the case, I resist him in those greater, may I not also vse those helpes which driue him away in the lesſer? I will if I can driue him away in all things.

Dan. Now the deuils are sent by the witches, and how they doe those bodily harmes, wee are not yet come vnto, and there lie two of the chiefe subtilties of the deuill in them, by which he deceiueth the multitude. But by occaſion we are fallen into the mention of remedie to driue them away. Because (I say) such as thus driue him away, know not the spirituall battell, much leſſe how to put on the whol armour of God to ouercome the deuil: Order doth require that we speak first of his sending, and then of those bodilie

C 3 harmes

harmes which he doth, & afterward of these meanes which are vsed to repell him. Let vs therefore step one step backe againe, if you agrée to the rest which I haue spoken.

M. B. With a good will: for so we shall omit no part. But I thought we had fullie agréd in this, that the witches do send their spirits, and doe manie harmes both vnto men and beasts: because we haue it confirmed by daylie experience: and vnlesse you will denie that which is manifest, I doubt not but we shall accorde in these.

Dan. I say the witches do send their spirits.

M.B. What shal we néd then to stand vpon that point in which we are agréd?

Dan. Yes, though we agree that they send them, yet we may dissent in diuers thinges about this sending. As first, tell me, whether doe you thinke that the witch or the Deuill is the seruaunt, which of them commaundeth, and which obeyeth?

M. B. How can I tell that? It is thought hee becommeth her seruaunt, and where she is displeased, and would be reuenged, she hyreth him for to doe it. The witches theselues haue confessed thus much: and for my part, I think no man can disprooue it.

Dan. They that doe the will of God are the childrē and seruants of God. And they which fulfill the lustes of the deuill, and obey him, are his childrē & his seruantes, Ioh. 8. verf. 44. Act. 13. verf. 10. Are they not?

M. B. I graunt all this?

Dan. The deuilles are the rulers of the darknesse of this world. Ephes. 6. ver. 12.

M. B. The text is plaine.

Dan. The darknesse of this world, is not meant of the darknesse of the night, which is but the shadow of the earth, but it is the spiritual darknes, which consisteth in the ignorance of God, in infidelitie, and in siune.

M. B. I am of your mind in this also.

Dan.

Dan. And doe you not thinke then that the deuill hath his throne, his dominion and kingdom in the hearts of ignorant blind infidels?

M. B. I must needs thinke he hath, the word of God doth force me thereunto: seeing he is the Prince of darkenesse.

Dan. And is there anie greater infidelitie and darknesse in anie, than in witches, conurers, and such as haue familiaritie with deuils?

M. B. I tak it they be the depest ouerwhelmed in darknesse and infidelitie of all other.

Dan. Lay all these thinges together which you confesse, and see whether it doth not follow vpon the same, that the witch is the vassall of the deuill, and not he her seruant; he is Lord and commaundeth, and she is his drudge and obeyeth.

M. B. Yea, although he be Lord, yet he is content to serue her turne, and the witches confesse, they call them forth and send them: and that they hire them to hurt such in their bodies, and in their cattell, as they bee displeased withall.

Dan. I am sorie you are so farre awrie, it is pitie any man should be in such errour, especiallie a man that hath learning, and should teach others knowledge.

M. B. Nay, I may returne this vpon you, for if you will denie this, it is but a follie to reason any further: I will neuer be driuen from that which I knowe: There was one olde mother W. of great T. which had a spirite like a a Weasill: she was offended highlie with one H. M. home she went, and called forth her spirite, which lay in a pot of woll vnder her bed, she willed him to goe plague the man: he required what she would giue him, and he would kill H. M. She said she would giue him a cocke, which shee did, and he went, and the man fell sicke with a great paine in his bellie, languished and died: the witch was arraigned,

C 4

condemned, and hanged, and did confesse all this.

Dan. I told you before that I do not deny these things, but you are deceiued about the doing: you marke not the cunning sleights of the deuill: Tel me, is not this the truth which S. Peter speaketh, that the deuil goeth about like a roaring lion, seeking whom he may deuoure. 1. Pet. 5.

M. B. What then?

Dan. What then? can you be so simple as to imagine that the deuill lieth in a pot of wooll, soft and warme, and stirreth not, but when he is hired and sent? The deuils conspire together in their worke, they bestirre them, and neuer take rest night nor day: they are neuer wearie, they be not a colde, they care not for lying soft: These be fooleries by which hee deceiueth the witches, and bewitcheth the mindes of many ignorant people: And whereas you say he is hired, it is but deceit: for, let me aske you two or three questions or more if need be.

M. B. What be your questions?

Dan. You say the witch commeth home angrie, who hath kindled this wrath in her heart but the deuill? Who inflameth her mind with malice, to be reuenged, and to doe mischiefe but the deuill? doth not he rule in her heart? Tell me what you thinke of this?

M. B. I muste needes confesse hee stirreth her vp to wrath and malice.

Dan. Then he lieth not at home in his pot of wooll: nor he is not hyred to this: hitherto she is his drudge, and obeyeth him, and not he her, being led by his suggestion. Then tell me, is not the deuill like a red or fierie dragon, Reuel. 12. burning in malice against God, and with all bloodie and cruell hatred that may be against men? And is he not farre readier vnto all mischiefe, than anie man or woman?

M. B. The deuill is more fierce than any man or woman; none can deny this.

Dan.

Dan. If none can deny this, and he be the worker of the wrath and malice in the heart of the witch; then what néedeth he to be hyred?he stirreth her vp,and if he would, he could turn her mind from sending him, and must he be hyred? doth he care for a cock or a chicken? Is he hungry or néedeth he somewhat to eat?

M.B. Nay,but it is thought he taketh those thinges to witnesse againſt the witch that ſhe is his.

Dan. Let it bee, there were somewhat in that which you speake, yet he hath a farre déeper reach, for the trueth is, hee woulde, and doeth perſwade the blind people, that he medleth litle, but when he is euen hyred and ſent, and that then his medling is but in such matters: And here-upon all is on a broyle againſt old women, which can any wayes be ſuſpected to be witches, as if they were the very plagues of the world, and as if all would be well, and ſafe from such harmes, if they were rooted out, and thus they fall a rooting out without all care: for it is thought that the witch which hath her spirits, is euen lyke a man which hath curſt dogges,which he may ſet vpon other mens cat-tell, which yet in the nature of dogs, would neuer ſtyrre but when they are bidden:and ſo the harmes do come from the man which oweth those dogs. They think that the country might be ryd of such spirits, if there were none to hoiſter them, or to ſet them a worke. They imagine that they and their cattell ſhould then goe ſafe. Alas poore creatures, how they be deluded? how litle do they vnderſtand the high prouidence of almighty God which is ouer all:

M. B. Doe you thinke then that witches ought not to be rooted out? or doe you thinke it were not much ſafety to the country from harmes,if it could be rid of them?

Dan. For the rooting out of witches, the Scripture is plaine. Thou ſhalt not ſuffer a witch to liue: but we are not yet come to that poynt. But whether they be to be rooted out that men may be ſafe from harmes, as the peo-

D ple

ple in fury and blindnesse imagine, that is next.

M.B. Men feele the smart and the harmes which they doe, and it is no maruell, though they be earnest to haue them rooted out, and a good riddance it were if the whole land could be set free from them.

Sam. Trulie M.B. I am of your mind, I wold they wer all hanged vp one against another: we should not (I hope) stand in such fear of their spirits. But I interrupt you too.

The wife. They that would not haue them hanged or burnt, I would they might euen witch them vnto hell. If I had but one fagot in the world, I would carry it a myle vpon my shoulders to burne a witch.

Dan. Well good woman, spare your fagot a while, and ease your shoulders, and let vs reason the matter a little further? I pray you let me aske you this question, doth the witch or the deuill the harme vnto men and cattell?

M.B. Why, the deuill doth it at their sending though I confesse it must needs be as you said, that the deuil worketh al in the mind of the witch, & moueth her to send him.

Dan. The deuill hath a kingdome, but it is in darkenesse and corruption of sinne. He hath no right nor power ouer Gods creatures, no not so much as to kill one flye, or to take one eare of corne out of anie mans barne, vnlesse power be giuen him. You know when Christ cast the deuils out of the man possessed, they aske leaue for to goe into the heard of swine. Then tell me, who giueth the deuill this power then, when the witch sendeth him, to kill or to lame man or beast? doth the witch giue it him? Do you think he had power to doe harme, but no mind till she moued him? Or doe you take it that her sending giueth him power, which he had not?

M.B. It is a question indeed worth the asking: For doubtlesse, the deuill hath not power vntill it be giuen him, to touch any creature, to hurt, or to destroy the body, but onely to tempt and to lead into sin: I am also sure that the

witch

witch cannot giue him power, but onlie God aboue.

Dan. Lay thefe two together then, that the deuill only hurteth, and that none can giue him power, neither man
nor woman, but only God, and tell me whether the people
be not wonderfully carried away in a rage. For, when as
they fhould confider, that the deuill is the Lordes executioner: And then finding that he hath any power giuen him
to moleft, to hurt and vexe them in theyr bodies or goods,
to know certainly it commeth from the Lord, and then ga-
ther from thence (as the trueth is) that the Lord is difplea-
fed with them for their offences. And fo feeke vnto him,
humbly crauing pardon and deliuerance from this enemy,
feeking to be armed with the mighty power of faith, to caft
him foorth, and to refift him, as the Lord willeth, 1. Pet. 5
Here is no fuch matter, no looking fo high among the people, but running deeper into errour, and into finne, as if the
witches did it, and that it commeth from their anger and
not from their owne finnes and infidelity, here is no repentance, no humbling themfelues by fafting and prayer,
but running for helpe vnto deuilles, vfing meanes which
thofe deuils by the cunning men & women appoint, fcrat-
ching and clawing, thirfting often after guiltles blood as
raging againft thofe whome they imagine to be witches,
which many times are not, becaufe they imagine, that if
there were no witches, ther fhould be no fuch plagues. As
if they had no foule finnes nor vnbeleefe, or that there re-
mayned not a iuft reuenging God to punifh, or as if he had
not the deuils ftill the executioners of his wrath.

M. B. Truly your wordes doe make me affrayd: for
I am euen guiltie of thofe thinges my felfe, if they be fo
grieuous, as you fet them out: and by Gods grace I wil
confider better of the matter: for I haue counfelled manie
to feek vnto thofe cunning folkes, and to vfe fuch helpes as
they prefcribe, and you fay, it is to feeke help at deuils. To
fee that point we fhal come anon: now I wold be refolued

about somewhat in your last speach; as namely, doe you cleare the witches, because God, and not they, giueth the deuil power, and doe you thinke that the deuils should kill men and their cattell, if they were not sent by witches? Should the harmes still follow, if there were no witches?

Dan. That I say God alone, and not the witches, giueth power vnto the deuils to plague and torment: it is so euident as that I suppose a man shall hardlie meete with anie man so grosse but will confesse it. But this doeth not cleare the witches at all; for their sinne is in dealing with deuils, and that they imagine that their Spirits do those harmes, requested and hyred by them: when as indeede the deuill, where he hath power giuen him to hurt, or where he knoweth death or grieuous diseases will follow either in man or beast, setteth the witch in a rage, and moueth her to send him. Concerning your other question, I say, we shall finde by the Scriptures, that if there were no witches at all, yet men should be plagued by the deuils in their bodies and goods. For touching the godly, the Lord doth vse Satan to afflict them in their bodies and in their goodes, for to trie their faith and patience: as the example of holie Job doeth testifie in ample maner. It were vile follie and brutish to affirme, that witches did set on the deuils to kill his children, and to plague his bodie. And I hold it no smal follie, for anie man to think that the Lord doeth not nowe scourge his children, at the least some of them, for their good, by the deuill. There is no doubt, but the deuil hauing power giuen him to afflict, vseth all the craft hee can, and will seek to be sent by the witch, and so yee will make it knowne, because it may seeme to bee not from God, but from the anger of a poore woman. And now touching the wicked, which prouoke God by their wicked sinnes and vnbeleefe, may we not read in the scriptures that an euill spirite was sent of God vnto king Saul, which did haunt and vexe him? Was this spirit sent by a witch? Or the de-

uils

uils in the Gospell, which entred into the hearde of swine
and drowned them? Did the Lord giue them power, and
send them, and shall we be so sottish as to thinke, that hee
sendeth not the deuill now against vngodly men, to plague
and to destroy them? As I said before, here is the deepe
craft of Satan, that he will couet to bee sent by witches,
whereas indeed God hath sent him, seeing none can sende
him but God. Againe, wee must consider that there bee
naturall causes in the bodies of men and beastes of grieuous tormentes and diseases, yea euen causes of death.
Nowe, they cannot be so secrete, but the deuill knoweth
them, and euen when they are like to take effect. Then doth
he plie it with the witch, setteth her in a furie, she sendeth
him, euen vpon this sending the man or the beast suddainlie and strangely are tormented, fall lame, or die. Then the
witch is suspected, examined, and confesseth that she killed
such a man, or such a mans cattell, or made them lame.
Here the people are set in a wonderfull maze and astonish-
ment, as if witches could plague men in their wrath. by
sending their spirits, because they confesse they did it, whē
their spirits doe lie and had no power, but the tormentes
came by naturall causes. And to driue the people into a
deeper madnes in this, & to make them beleeue, that strange
and suddaine torments and languishing diseases come by
witches, he hath his other sort of witches, the cunning men
and women, which tell euen vpon his worde, which you
know is to be trusted, that they be bewitched, that they bee
haunted with fayries, and that ther be thus many witches
therabout, in euerie town some.

    M. B. That is most true no doubt, which you speake,
I doe not for my part knowe how to gainsay any one point
thereof. Only I wonder at the craftinesse of the deuils in
these things, that where they haue power graunted vnto
them to hurt, they wil be sent by the witches, as if they did
it hired by them, and that you say where harmes doe follow

low men vpon naturall causes,that they can make shew as though they did them.But are you of this mind,that there should be as manie or all those harmes done by deuilles, if there were no witches,as there be now? Although I must needs confesse,that the witches can giue the deuil no pow-er,nor he can take none by their sending: yet may it not bee that God giueth them power oftener because of those wit-ches dealing with them , than if there were no witches at all?

Dan. The craftinesse of deuils is such,as without the light of Gods worde, the wisest men vnder heauen muste nædes be deceiued thereby. We sæ there be some men so dæp in subtilties and can carie matters so close , that men can not discerne them:how much more the deuilles, which are exceedingly subtill,& craftie aboue the subtillest men? the question which you aske is(in my iudgment)somwhat hard: But this is vndoubted,that if the Lord God do giue vnto the deuils oftener power to hurt because of the wit-ches,I meane because the deuils doe deale by such instru-ments,it is in his heauie iudgment against the wickednes of the people,which despise the true and heauenlie light of his word. As S. Paule (prophecying of the comming of the great Antichrist)sheweth,that because men did not re-ceiue the loue of the trueth, God gaue the deuill power by Antichrist and his ministers, to seduce by lying signes and wonders. Indæd,I will not say that for the witch the de-uill hath power giuen him, but for the wickednesse of the people , which deserue that by witches the deuill shoulde haue power to seduce them further. Here yet we muste take hæde of the common errour which a multitude are ca-ried so hedlong withall,that they can by no means sæ, that God is prouoked by their sinnes to giue the deuill such in-struments to work withall, but rage against the witch, e-uen as if she could do all.

M. B. Surelie, I should bee a wretch to deny, that
God

God giueth the Deuilles power to plague and to seduce because of mens wickednes ; but yet I would knowe whether a godly faythfull man or woman may not bee bewitched? Wée sée the deuill had power giuen him ouer Iob?

Dan. This example of Iob is not fit to prooue that a godly man may be bewitched, séeing the deuill is not sayde to deale by witches against him, but it doeth prooue, that not only the godlie, but euen the most godly (as holy Iob, who had none like him vpon earth) may for their triall be giuen into the handes of Satan to be afflicted and tempted. And as I said, where Satan hath power granted him of God, to strike with bodily plagues any of the godly, for the triall of their fayth and patience, he will couet, if he can bring it about, to bee sent by some witch, and to haue it knowne that he was sent. But the faithfull are to turne theyr eies from the witch, and to deale with God, for from him the matter commeth. When they be tried, the Lord in his good time will deliuer them depending vpon him, to their great prayse and glory, euen as valiant souldiers. It is therefore, of no great force, whether Satan come from the witch against the godlie, or whether he haue no witch to deale by: ouercome thou the deuill, and thou ouercommest all. Indéed among the more ignorant sort he preuayleth much, when he toucheth those which imbrace the liuely word as sent from a witch. For many nowe doe euen quake and tremble, and their faith doth stagger. Hath hée power (thinke they) ouer such as be cunning in the scriptures, then what are they the better for their profession? the witch is on their bones as well as vpon others. By this it might séeme, and so they take it, that other helpes and remedies are to be sought than by the scriptures. And so they run and séeke help where they ought not.

M. B. Then I pray you, though I be already perswaded it is naught to séeke to these cunning men for help against witches, yet let vs conferre a little of that. There

be

be diuers things which haue perſuaded me to thinke marueilous well of them, and euen as of ſuch as God hath giuen wiſedome and ſkill vnto, euen for to doe much good.
For we ſee many receiue help by them, and are deliuered
from the plagues which come by deuils. And firſt, I wold
know how they can bee ſo earneſt againſt witches, if they
deale with the deuill, and ſo be inced witches themſelues?
how can they haue any mind in charity to doe good, to take
pitie vpon ſuch as be in miſery? Or how will Satan driue
forth Satan? For they no doubt, driue out deuilles out of
ſome.

    Dan. I would come to aunſwere your queſtions tou-
ching the ſeeking help at the hands of cunning men or women, but tell me firſte, are you reſolued touching the ſending of the ſpirits, and touching the harms that are done?
Me think you ſlip too ſuddainly from theſe points?

    M. B. I cannot tell whether I vnderſtand your mea-
ning in euery thing, but ſure, I haue bene in error greatly I muſt needs confeſſe. And if you pleaſe, we may ſtande
ſomewhat longer in theſe queſtions.

    Sam. Indeed it is my deſire that you woulde ſpeake a
litle playner of theſe poyntes: for I haue marked well all
your talke, and cannot well conceiue of the laſt things you
dealt in. With your leaue *M. B.* I would aſke two or
three queſtions of my friend. Here was but ſeuen miles
hence at W. H. one M. the man was of good wealth, and
well accounted of among his neighbours. He pined away
with ſickneſ halfe a yeare, and at laſt died. After hee was
dead, his wife ſuſpected ill dealing: ſhe went to a cunning
man, I know not where, and deſired to know whereof her
huſband died. He told her that her huſband died of witcherie: he aſked her if ſhe did not ſuſpect any therabout. She
ſayd there was one woman which ſhe did not like, one mother W. her huſband and ſhe fell out, and he fell ſick within two dayes after, and neuer recouered again. He ſhewed
                                        her

her the woman as plaine in a glasse, as we see one another,
and in the very apparell she went in at that hower, for shee
ware an old red cappe with corners, such as women were
wont to weare; and in that she appeared in the glasse: Hee
taught her how she might bring her to confesse. Well, she
followed his counsell, went home, caused her to be apprehended and caried before a Iustice of peace. He examined
her so wisely, that in the end she confessed shee killed the
man. She was sent to prison, she was arraigned, condemned, and executed: And vpon the ladder shee seemed very
penetent, desiring all the world to forgiue her. She said
she had a spirit in the likenes of a yellow dun catte. This
catte came vnto her, as she said, as she sat by her fire, when
she was fallen out with a neighbour of hers, and wished
that the vengeance of God might light vpon him and his.
The catte bad her not be affraid, she wold do her no harme:
She had serued a dame fiue yeares in Kent, that was now
dead, and if she would, she would be her seruant. And wheras, said the Cat, such a man hath misused thee, if thou wilt
I will plague him in his cattell. She sent the Cat, she killed three hogs and one Cow. The man suspecting, burnt a
pig aliue, and as she said, her cat wold neuer go thither any
more. Afterward she fel out with that M. she sent her Cat,
who told her, that she had giuen him that, which hee should
neuer recouer: and indeed the man died. Now doe you not
thinke the woman spake the trueth in all this? Would the
woman accuse her selfe falsely at her death? Did not the
Cat become her seruant? Did not she send her? Did shee
not plague and kill both man and beaste? What shoulde a
man thinke of this?

   Dan. You propounde a particular example, and let
vs examine euery thing in it touching the witch, for the
womans fact that went to the wise man, wee are not yet
come to that point. You say the Cat came to her when she
was in a great rage with one of her neighbours, and did

curſe, wiſhing the vengeance of God to fall vpon him and his.

Sam. She ſaid ſo indæde. I heard her with mine own ears, for I was at the execution.

Dan. Then tel me who ſet her in ſuch a deuiliſh rage, ſo to curſe & banne, as to wiſh that the vengeance of God might light vpon him and his? did not the Cat?

Sam. Trulie I thinke the Deuil wrought that in her.

Dan. Uerie well, then you ſæ the Cat is the beginner of this play.

Sam. Cald you it a play? It was no play to ſome.

Dan. Indeed the witch at laſt had better haue wrought hard, than bene at her play. But I meane Satan did play the Iugler : For, doth he not offer his ſeruice? Doth he not moue her to ſend him to plague the man? Tell me, is ſhe ſo forward to ſend, as he is to be ſent? Or doe you not take it, that he ruleth in her heart, and euen wholly directeth it to this matter?

Sam. I am fully perſwaded he ruleth her heart.

Dan. Then was ſhee his drudge, and not he her ſeruant, he needeth not to be hired nor intreated, for if her hart were to ſend him any where, vnto ſuch as he knoweth hee cannot hurt, nor ſeeth how to make any ſhewe that he hurteth them, he can quickly turne her from that. Wel, the cat goeth and killeth the man, certain hogs and a Cow: howe could ſhe tell that the Cat did it?

Sam. How could ſhe tell? why he told her man, and the law and heard that he loſt his cattell.

Dan. The Cat would lie, would ſhe not? for they ſay ſuch cattes are lyers.

Sam. I doe not truſt the Cats wordes, but becauſe the thing fell out ſo.

Dan. Becauſe the hogges and the Cow died, are you ſure the Cat did kil them, might they not die of ſome naturall cauſes as you ſæ both men and beaſts are well, and die

ſud-

suddainlie?

Sam. That were strange, if they should die of naturall causes, and fall out so fit at the time after he was sent?

Dan. It is not straunge at all, as marke what I tell you and you shall easily sée. There bee naturall causes of tortures and griefe, of lamenes, and of death in the bodies of men and beastes, which lie so hid and secrete, that the learneddest Physitians can not espie them, but the deuill séeth them, and can coniecture very neere the time, when they will take effect. Then doeth hee plye it, to bring the matter about that it may séeme he did it. If hee haue any witch to deale by, he stirreth vp some occasion to set her in a rage with that partie: and then he will be sent, and telleth her he doeth it. If he haue no witch to deale by, yet hee will set debate betwéene the partie and some other, whom he may bring into suspition, as his greatest desire is to haue innocent bloud shed.

Sam. Here is a matter brought about indéed, how could the Cat doe all this?

Dan. I told you before, that the deuilles worke together, and can spéedilie and most craftilie compasse thinges, which are farre beyond the reach of mans capacitie. But sometime the deuill hath power giuen him to plague and doth the harme. Admit he had power giuen him, and did kill the cattell of this man: let vs come nowe to that, who think you, gaue him the power for to strike and kill? Did the witch giue him the power, or the Lord God?

Sam. Nay surely, the witch cannot giue him power.

Dan. Did he receiue power after she sent him?

Sam. That cannot I tell.

Dan. Thē mark a litle: he hath power giuē him to plague this man in his goods: he wil do it, but he will doe it craftily. The Lord gaue him power ouer the goods of holie Job: he worketh by instruments, for he stirreth vp the Sabeis, and they take away his Oxen, and his Asses: he raiseth vp

also the Chaldeis, and they cary away his Camels, Iob. 1.
Euen so, hauing power to strike, he wil be sent by a witch,
he could doo it without her, but he gayneth much that way,
as we shall sée when wee come to speake of the remedyes
which men seeke.

Sam. I wonder then that the man neuer had more hurt
after he had burnt his pig aliue:

Dan. O man, the Deuill can abide no roast meate, nor
no fire, he is affraide, if they fall a roasting, that they will
roast him. If they run at him with a spit red hot, they gas-
ter him so sore, that his dame shal go her self, if she will he
will come no more there. But of these thinges we are to
speake afterward in their place.

Sam. You make the deuill wonderfull subtill.

Dan. He is so subtill and full of all craft and sleight,
that no earthly creature can escape from being seduced by
him, without the light of Gods heauenly word. But let vs
come now to the other man, whom the witch confessed shee
killed by her Cat.

Sam. Yea, that me thinketh is more than the other,
the woman was told by the cunning man that her husband
was killed by witcherie. The witch confessed so much at
her death. The Cat told the witch, that she killed him.

Dan. Here be a companie of credible persons to be beleeued: the cunning man saith the man was bewitched to
death. Who told him that?

Sam. His spirite that maketh the witch appeare in the
glasse.

Dan. That same Spirite, what doe you take him to
be, an Angell, or a Deuill?

Sam. Some of the cunning men say, they haue Moses
or Elias, or the Spirite of some holy man.

Dan. The Deuill can turne himselfe into the liknes
of an Angell of light. For they that doe thinke the cunning
men and women deale with any other Spirite than Sa-

tan

tan, haue no vnderstanding. Satan saith, the man was witched to death.

Sam. Satan saith so, he is not to bee beleeued, but the witch confesseth it was so.

Dan. Who told the witch?

Sam. Her Cat that she sent.

Dan. What is the Cat, a deuill? then remember the prouerbe, aske his fellow if he be a theefe. All the matter resteth vpon the testimony of deuils, and they not put to their oath. Wee will not ground vpon mans testimonie without an oath, and must we beleeue the bare worde of deuils?

Sam. Do you thinke then that the man was not killed by witcherie?

Dan. It may be the Lord had giuen Satan power to plague the man in his bodie, and then he vnder a colour would be sent by a witch. But it is most like that his bodie did languish and pine of naturall causes, which the deuill did know, and so would be sent, and seeme to do all, when as indeed he had no power to touch him. For, although the Lord giue the deuill power, to strike some in their bodies for their haynous sinnes, yet the most which the witches thinke their spirits doe kill at their request, doe die of naturall diseases.

Sam. Then it seemeth the witches are deceiued, and mocked, when he maketh them beleue he doeth kill and plague when hee doeth not. And againe in this, where he hath power giuen him of God, to strike man or beast, hee could doe it, and would without the witch, and so vseth the witch for a collour to draw on worse matters.

Dan. I am glad you take my meaning so right: for, thinke deeply of the matters, and you shall see it must needs be so.

Sam. I interrupted M. B. I pray you goe forward now to the rest.

E 3   Dan.

Dan. Our matter which we come vnto nowe, is the helpe and remedie that is sought for against witches at the hands of cunning men. And now if it please you to propound your questions, I will answere to them the best I can.

M. B. Nay truly, I see already all is naught, but yet I will obiect those things which haue caried me awrie. I take it a man is to seek remedy against euils, & I thought it was euen a gift that God gaue vnto those whom we cal cunning men, that they did very much good by. When a thing is lost, when a thing is stollen, many goe to them, and they help them to it. I did know where the Communion cup was stollen: the Churchwardens rode to a wise man, he gaue them direction what night, and where they should stand, and the party that had stollen it should come thither, and confesse he had it: and certainly they had it againe. I did know one that had a child of fiue yeares old, a gyrle, it was taken piteouslie: the father was in great heauinesse, and knew not what to doe: some gaue him counsell to goe to a woman which dwelt ten miles from him, and to carie some of the clothes which the child lay inthe did so, the woman told him that his child was bewitched, and if hee did not seeke remedie in time, the childe would be lost: Shee bad him take some olde clothes, and let the child lie in them all night, and then take and burne them: and he should see by the burning, for if they did burne black, that shewed the child was bewitched, and she said further, that doubtlesse the witch would come thither: he followed her aduice, and sure as we be here, there came an old woman in, which he suspected, euen while they were burning, and made an errand: the man made no more adoe, but euen laid his clowthes vpon her and clawed her vntill the blood ranne down her cheeks, and the child was well within two dayes after. I could tell you of a stranger thing, but I haue it but by report, but yet indeed by very credible report: There was

a butcher by his trade that had a boy to his sonne, his name
was John, grieuous sores did breake forth vpon him: they
laid salues, and none woulde cleaue for to draw or to ease
them. The father making his moane to a friend of his, he
told him whether he should goe to a verie skilfull man : he
did goe, and being demanded whom he suspected, she was
shewed him in a glasse, an old woman that dwelt not farre
from him in an house alone: he told the cunning man, that
the woman had shut vp her dore, & was gone from home
out of the shyre, and so he could not tell how to come by her.
he told him a way how he, should fetch her home. Cut off
the hair (said he) of the boyes head, and put it in a cloath
and burne it, and I warrant you she wil come home with al
the spæd she can. Burne it abroade, burne it not in a chim-
ney, for if you doe, it will make you all affraide. The man
went home and did this. The woman came home with
all spæde, came to his house, came to the boy, and saide,
John, scratch me, hee scratched her vntil the blood followed, and whereas before nothing would draw his soares,
they healed of themselues. What should a man thinke of
such things ?

Dan. You tell of some, which haue receiued help from
the hands of cunning men: And no doubt there may infinit
examples be brought. Some haue lost, some haue thinges
stollen from them, some are vexed in their bodies: They
come by the things againe which were lost or stollen, they
are taught to doe certain things, and are eased from their
griefs. But this we must first knowe, they receiue their
helpe, if it deserue the name to be called help, from the deuill. And do you thinke a man may lawfullie seek helpe at
the hands of the deuill?

M.B. Some are perswaded that they doe not sæke
helpe at the hand of deuils, when they goe to the wise men :
but that it is a gift which God hath giuen them, euen to do
good withall.

Dan. I doe verilie thinke that manie of the people are so perswaded: but what reason is there for it? Doeth God by his Spirit tell where the thing is which is lost, or stollen? Is it an Angell from heauen, or the soule of some man that is dead, which appeareth in the Chrystall, or in the glasse, and sheweth the image of the partie which hath stollen, or that is a witch?

M. B. I had rather heare what you thinke touching these things, than shew what I haue thought.

Dan The deuils did make the heathen people beleue that they were goddes, and so procured that they shoulde worship them with diuine worship. Through their craftines they had many wayes to establish this: they conueied themselues into images, and out of them gaue answeres, when they wer demanded, herein they vsed great craft, for whereas they could not tell what should fall out, they framed the oracle in such sort as it was doubtfull, and might be taken both waies: and so looke which part it fell out on, that seemed and was taken to be the meaning of the gods. If they did know how things would fal out indeed, as they did know sundry things touching the kingdomes and monarchies of the world, by the writings of the Prophetes, and diuers things by coniectures, as the deuill could tell Saul he should be slaine, because he saw God had cast him off, and the hearts of the Israelits fainted, and the Philistims were full of courage, those they would tell plainelie. Also they did conuey themselues into the bodies of men and women, and vtter thinges which semed very diuine, such (as I am perswaded) were the Prophetisses the Sibylles among the heathen. Such was the maide at Philippos, which is mentioned in the Actes of the Apostles, which brought great gain vnto her maisters by deuining, out of whom Paule cast the deuill. This maide could tell of things lost, of things stollen, and such like, and great resort there was vnto her, as men had neede, or desired to see the strangenesse of the matter.

M. B. Let me interrupt you a litle. The deuill can not be in all places at once: how could he then, remaining in the maide, tell what was done in places farre off? howe can the deuill tel where the thing lost or stollen is, which is not only farre off, but hidden? how can he shewe the image of the thiefe or witch? Can he sit and beholde all thinges a farre off, and in secrete?

Dan. We may not ascribe vnto Deuils that they can be in all places at once, or sit in one place and beholde all things done a farre off. But they ioyne together in this speciall worke, to set vp their kingdome, and to drawe the people after them, to seeke helpe at their handes, and so to worship them. Some of them be in one place, and some in another, and from all places doe stir vp the faithlesse people to run for helpe to those cunning men, and then they make the relation, for they goe thither also, they know the thiefe whome they moued to the theft, and can make resemblance of his face and apparell: they can tell where things be that are hid, hauing had a finger in the matter. And thus one spirite, as it doeth seeme, telleth things spoken and done farre off, but it is otherwise, there be manie that doe it, which resort from all the places where the things are done.

M. B. I am satisfied touching this point. You were shewing howe the deuils did deale among the heathen out of the Idols, and out of men and women.

Dan. Yea, and they haue subtillie wound themselues in againe among Christians. For vsing witches as their instruments, they make them beleue that they doe manie harmes sent by them, which they do not, and whereas they haue power giuen them by God to afflict, they will seeme to doe it at the wrath and displeasure of the witch, she must send him, the matter must one way or other appeare, eyther he will seeme euen compelled by force of such as do ad-

iure

iure him, to confesse that such a woman oʒ such a man sent
him, oʒ els the witch muſt confeſſe ſo much. Then the peo=
ple deuiſe how they may be ſafe againſt the witch, there is
running to the wiſardes to learne what they ſhould doe.to
withſtand the furie of the witch, that ſhe ſend not to them,
oʒ if ſhe haue ſent, how they may expell her ſpirit, and kæp
her from ſending him againe : this is it which the deuill
would haue: foʒ now he vttereth all his wares: he teacheth
by theſe cunning men and women, many hoʒrible abho=
minations, and foule abuſes of the name of God, by which
they are made beleeue, that they haue remedie againſt the
deuils ſent by the witches , and that they are cured from
their harmes.

   M. B. I doe not ſæ how any man can indæd iuſtifie,
oʒ maintaine, that the ſpirits which appeare vnto them in
the Chʒiſtall, oʒ in the glaſſe, oʒ water, oʒ that any way do
ſpeake, and ſhewe matters vnto them , be holy Angels, oʒ
the ſoules of excellent men, as of Moſes, Samuel, Dauid,
and others, though I haue heard that the cunning men,
take them to be ſuch, and thinke they deale by them againſt
deuils.

   Dan. It is no matter what Satans vaſſals are made
to beleeue by his ſubtil ſleights: it is moſt abhominable foʒ
any Chʒiſtian man, euer to let it enter into his thought,
that they doe any thing by the power oʒ wiſdome of the ho=
lie Ghoſt, by any Angel oʒ good ſpirit, oʒ that they doe any
thing againſt the deuill, which woʒke by the intelligence
which they haue from euill ſpirits: therfoʒs hold this, that
they ſeeke vnto deuils, which run vnto thoſe ſouthſayers.

   M. B. I am perſwaded indæd that they ſeek vnto de=
uils, but I would ſee ſome reaſon foʒ it out of Gods woʒd.

   Dan. Touching all ſpirituall matters, as to be ar=
med with power againſt deuils, and to know how to auoid
the daungers which they bʒing , we are no where to ſeeke,
and to learne but of our moſt bleſſed Loʒde God. And of
him

him we cannot learn, but by his holy word, for in it he hath opened vnto vs all his whole will. And therefore, where the Lorde commaundeth the people of Israell by Moses, Deut. 18. that they should not when they came into the land, learn to do according to the abhominations of those heathen, reckoning vp sundry kinds of such as were Satans instruments which he vsed to seduce the multitude, by deuinations, by obseruing of times, by augurie, by iuglings with the helpe of the deuill, by vsing familiar Spirits, spirits of deuination, and seeking to the dead : he setteth downe also the remedie, shewing first, that he woulde cast out those nations because they harkened vnto the southsayers, and deuiners, pronouncing that euerie one which doth those things, is an abhomination to the Lorde, willing his people that they should not harken to such, but that they should hearken vnto him : And then Moses saith, A Prophet shall the Lord thy God raise vp vnto thee from among you of thy brethren like vnto me, him shal ye heare.

M. B. Then you proue by that place, that we muste seeke only to God, and not to such as work by meanes besides his words.

Dan. If you read that place, Deut. 18. and mark euery thinge well, you shall see it doeth not onely proue that they seeke vnto Deuilles, which runne to these cunning men and women : because the Prophetes which God hath raysed vp to declare the Lords will, commaund vs not to doe such things: but also declareth that they bee an abhomination to the Lorde that vse them, or that seeke vnto them.

M. B. I see then it is not onelie a sinne, but a moste horrible sinne, to seeke vnto them. Alas, many do not think that they seeke vnto deuilles, when they goe for helpe vnto them for thinges stollen, or for helpe and remedie against witches.

Dan,

Dan. No doubt many refuse to hear the voyce of God, to be instructed by him: they despise his word, and therfore they be giuen vp to hearken vnto Deuilles. Such as haue sought vnto any of these that worke by the deuill, and new come to see their offence, ought to shew repentance for the same, not as for a light sinne. It is no small abhomination to goe for helpe vnto the deuill: It is to set him in Gods place, and to honour him as God. It riseth of infidelity and distrust of help from God, as we may see in the example of king Saule, who finding no answere nor comforte from God, whome he had so wickedly disobeyed, went to a witch. The heathen man saide, *Flectere si nequeo Superos, Acheronta mouebo.* It I cannot intreat the goddes, I will downe among the deuils.

M. B. Nay, doubtles there can be no defence made for such séeking help at their hands, which deale with familiar spirits, but I muse at diuers thinges, as this for one, how the cunning men, if they deale by the power of the deuill, should vse such good wordes, and will them that come vnto them to doe all in the name of Christ, teaching them to vse words and sentences of the scriptures.

Dan. O sir, here lieth the déep subtiltie of Satan, how should the people be seduced to follow him, if he should not vse great cunning to couer matters, as if deuils were driuen out, and harmes cured that are done by them, euen through the name and mightie power of God. Herein also lyeth a more foule abhomination, and that is the abusing and horrible prophaning of the most blessed name of God, and the holie Scriptures vnto witcheries, charmes, and coniurations, and vnto all deuillish artes. Such an one is haunted with a fayrie, or a spirit: he must learne a charme compounded of some straunge speaches, and the names of God intermingled, or weare some part of S. Johns Gospell or such like. So against the thiefe, against the deuill sent by the witch, thel ike is practized. What can Satan
de-

desire more, than that holie thinges should be thus abused? There is adoe to get him into the glasse, to get him into the Chrystall, to get him into the basen of water: there is a doe to binde him, as it were by the name & power of Christ to tell this thing or that thing. The coniurer hee bindeth him with the names of God, and by the vertue of Christes passion and resurrection, & so maketh him serue his turne: And all is his owne worke, for he is not constrayned, nor bound, but seeketh thus to haue God blasphemed. O (sayth the simple man) this is a good woman, shee speaketh of God, and of Christ, and doth all in his name: they be good wordes which she hath taught me to vse: and what hurt can there be in vsing good wordes? Alas poore man, what case are they in which must learne good wordes of the deuill? It is not the speaking of good wordes, or the wearing some part of the scriptures, that defendeth from deuils, therein lieth the craft of satan, to haue those holy thinges so foullie abused, and that men may put trust in wordes and senten-ces pronounced, but the deuilles are withstood onlie by the power of faith, where the holie scriptures are written in the heart, & the soule armed with the power of them. From this Satan draweth men by his soothsayers, teaching them other helpes: For the naming of God, or the senten-ces of scripture bindeth not satan, when wee reade he can vtter them.

M. B. Then howe can the deuill beare such a pitifull minde, as to help those that bee in miserp? For many haue helpe by these cunning men. The deuill is cruell and bent wholly to doe hurt, and that is it which perswadeth manie that things are done euen by the power of God.

Dan. The deuils be as pitifull as a greedy hungrie li-on that roareth after his pray, and as a fierce Dragon, all burning with wrath and bloody malice: they make shew of doing good vnto men, only of a most cruel and murtherous purpose, euen to draw men deeper into the pit of hell with

them,

them. For if they can help the bodie a litle, it is to win both bodie and soule vnto eternall damnation. Where satan offereth his help, it is more to be feared, than where he manifestly impugneth, and seeketh apparantly to hurt.

*M.*B. But this then is more strange, if they doe not deale by the power of God, but by the power of the deuill, when they driue out deuils from hurting, howe one deuill should driue out another. Our sauiour saith, that satan doth not driue out satan, for then his kingdom should bee deuided and could not stand.

Dan. It is most certaine that satan doth not driue out satan : for our sauiour hath shewed the reason of the contrarie. One deuill is readie to further the worke of another: but in no wise to expel or to hinder one another.

*M.*B. There is it which maketh me to muse : we sée the deuill driuen out, and doeth not returne againe, and if it be not wrought by the power of deuilles, as you say it cannot, then must it néeds be by the power of God,

Dan. The Deuill is driuen out, neither by the power of the deuill, nor yet by the power of God, in these that are healed by cunning men.

*M.*B. I like this worst of al the speach which I heard you vtter yet: For if satan be not driuen out neither by the power of satan, nor by the power of God, what other power is there to driue him out? If you can shewe a third power to expell him, it is more than euer I heard of.

Dan. There néedeth not a thirde power to expell him, for he is not driuen out at all.

M.B. I told you before, if you denie that to be, which all experience doth shewe, then is it no reasoning. There be examples in many places, and daylie it is séene, that the deuill is driuen out of some possessed, that where he did vexe and torment men in their bodies, and in their cattle, they haue remedie against him.

Dan. I doe not denie but that some which are possessed

sed and tormented by Satan, haue release : but yet the de=
uill is not cast foorth by those means, but ceaseth willingly
euen to establish men in errour , and in most wicked pro=
phaning of the name of God, and worshipping of himselfe,
and so entreth deeper into them.

M. B. I beseech you let me heare how that is, that you
say he ceaseth of his owne accord. Will he let goe his hold
willingly and of his owne accord , where he hath it vpon a=
ny man : Doth he not desire to doe hurt?

Dan. He doeth not let goe his hold which he hath vpon
any man, but indeed taketh faster holde when hee seemeth to
be cast foorth and doth greater hurt: for tell me whose deuise
is the coniuration?

M. B. I am out of doubt that coniuration is the de=
uice of the deuill.

Dan. Then tell me, hath the deuill deuised and taught
a way to bind himselfe, or to cast foorth himselfe ?

M. B. That I suppose he would neuer doe.

Dan. Indeed if we wil imagine that the deuil is becom
an old foole, we may think he wold teach that which should
bind and cast foorth himselfe: but the scripture calleth him
the old serpent : he deuised and taught coniuration, there=
fore coniuration doth not cast him foorth. Yet he seemeth to
be bound by the coniurer, yea euen by the name of God, and
by the power of the passion of Christ. The coniurer seemeth
by the same power to driue him out of a man possessed,
whose body he doth vex & torment. And he ceaseth willingly
to torment the bodie, to establish coniuration , & so to draw
men quite from God, euen to worship and to follow him=
selfe, and seeke all helpes at his hands. Euen so when men
are tormented in their bodies , or plagued in their cattell
by the deuill, and seeke vnto the cunning men and women,
following the way that they prescribe vnto them, and haue
eale in their bodies, and no more harme among their cattell, Satan doth not giue place as forced, but ceaseth to do

those

those bodilie harmes, that he may fullie win vnto himselfe both bodie and soule. If they should not seeme to bee expelled, how should men be drawn to seek help at their handes which deale by him: how should witches and coniurers be drawne on most horriblie to pollute and blaspheme the glorious name of God?

M. B. Then I see they buy their help deer which haue it at the handes of these cunning men.

Dan. Yea, what can be bought more deare, than that which is with the losse of soule and bodie for euer, by running from God after deuils?

M. B. What shoulde a man thinke then touching all other which deale not with the deuill and yet haue certaine waies to finde out witches, and to vnwitch that which they haue done?

Dan. Although they deale not directly by the deuill, I meane they haue no familiar spirites that speake vnto them yet they deale by deuillish deuises, which are also an abhomination to the Lord. For all those seuerall sortes of witches which the Lord rehearseth, Deut. 18. did not deale directlie with deuils. For some were obseruers of times, which had their luckie dayes and their vnluckie dayes, and so their howers. If they goe to buy or to sell, they chuse their hower to set foorth in. Some dealt by the intralles of beasts, and by the flying of birds, by meeting with an hare, or a foxe, and on which hand, & a thousand such like. Some deal with the Siue and a paire of sheeres, vsing certaine wordes: Some vse a charme for the tooth ach, another for the ague, and for stopping the bleeding at the nose, also their spell for the theefe, and a thousande such like, when butter will not come,' when cheese will not runne, nor Ale worke in the fatte: These would seeme of all others to haue witches in the greatest detestation, and in the meane time worke by the deuill themselues, and may bee termed witches.

M. B.

M. B. We doe count them witches which haue their spirits, we doe not take them to be witches which doe but vse those things which the cunning men haue taught. For they doe not mean to doe any thing by the deuill. Me thinketh therefore it is hard to call them witches.

Dan. Take the name of witchcraft for all that dealeth by the power and deuices of the deuill. No doubt some are more horrible than other of the seuerall sortes of witches, yet the lightest of them be abhominations before the Lord, as we are taught, *Deut.* 18. and the ignorance doeth not excuse. For what though the witch suppose it is the soule of Moses, which appeareth in his Chrystal, is he not therfore a witch: Your neighbour, whose butter wold not come, which heat a spit red hoat and thrust into the creame, vsing certaine wordes, doth thinke she did by the power of God fray away the deuill, is she not therefore a witch, dealing with that which the deuil, and not God hath taught? Is she not a witch also in seeking help at deuils? They which did burne the cloaths which their child lay in, to know by the burning blacke whether it were bewitched, and to bring the witch thither, dealt altogether by the power and direction of the deuill, & so in scratching, for God hath taught no such things, then are they not witches? By whose instruction, and by whose power was the witch fetched home at the burning of the hair of the butchers sonne you spake of? Was not all done by the power of Satan, and by his instruction? Are not they then which practize the thinges the Disciples of witches, & so indeed very witches? Those which haue their charmes, and their night spels, what can they be but witches? I might reckon vp her that dealeth with the siue and the sheares, and a number of such trumperies, in all which the most holie name of God is polluted, and if any thing be done, it is done wholly by the effectuall working of Satan. God hath giuen naturall helps, and those we may vse, as from his hand against naturall

G. diseas

diseases, but things besides nature he hath not appointed, especiallie, they be ridiculous to driue away deuilles and diseases.

M. B. Now you speak of naturall things, we see there be great secretes in nature : the Adamant draweth Iron vnto it. And why m ay there not be some force in these na-turall things then?

Dan. No doubt there be great secrets in nature, which the skilfull Physitians, and naturall Philosophers do find out. As the hanging of some thinge about the necke, may haue force to driue away an ague , the wearing of some thing may haue such vertue to deliuer from the cramp, and such like. And from these Satan doeth take occasion to bring in his trumperies, and curious deuiles. As because there be secretes in nature, a ring is curiouslie framed ac-cording to the signes in the firmament, this is tied to a thread, and let downe into a basen or cup of water, and wil shew great things. Because there be secretes in nature, a horsshoo must be heat red hot, and then put into a kettle see-thing vpon the fire to driue away the witches spirite. Also he that hath his cattle bewitched, burneth some liue thing, as hogge or henne, to driue out the deuill. Can these natu-rall thinges expell deuils? Nay, they play the rancke wit-ches, which burne any thing for to expell deuils: for, hath God taught to doe anie such thing? Doe they burne the thing to God, or is it as a verie burnt sacrifice to the De-uill? In the time of the law burnt sacrifices were offred to God: the deuill among the heathen drewe the like to him-selfe: And now by his sleight he doth after some sort procure the same at their hands , which professe to be Christians, and thus worshipping him, he ceaseth from hurting their bodies, or their cattell, as gaining a greater matter.

M. B. If it be so (as I am not able to gainsay it) then be there multitudes in all places which are guiltie of sorce-rie and witchcraft. For I see many deale in matters by

the

the help and power of the deuill, which are perswaded o-
therwise. But I meruaile much at diuers things touching
the help which men haue by deuils. Let vs conferre a little
about them. The deuill doeth know things past, & things
present, but God onelie doth know what shall bee done in
the time to come. If these cunning men doe deale with no
further power, than the power of the deuill, howe can they
tell so right what shall come to passe?

Dan. It is peculiar to God alone, to know what shall
come to passe hereafter. But the Lord God hath reuealed
by his Prophetes, and Apostles many thinges that after
should be fulfilled. Satan can giue a nere coniecture when
these come to be fulfilled. Hee is a most subtill obseruer of
thinges, and will gesse at many: but especially, where hee
hath power giuen him to worke and to bring any matter
about, he can and will tell it aforehand. Finally, God in his
iust iudgement giueth him power to seduce the wicked.

M. B. I pray you open your meaning more fully.

Dan. Uery well: In which haue you any doubt?

M. B. I take it the Deuill gesseth at things which are
prophecied, and is a sharpe obseruer of causes. But you
said he telleth what shall be where he worketh that which
he foretelleth: giue some example for this.

Dan. There needeth no better example, than that
which you tolde of the Churchwardens that went to the
cunning man, to knowe the theefe which had stollen their
communion cuppe. It may be sayd, where the cunning
man bad them go to such a place, such a night, and at such
an hower, and thither shall come he that stole the cup, how
could the deuill tell, if it were a night or two after, that he
should come to that place, and at that hower? You muste
note what power the deuill hath in the mind of a theefe. He
stirred him vp to steale the cup. He stirred vp the Churchwardens to seeke to the cunning witch. Hee nameth the
place and the time, whether, and when he would moue the

heart

heart of the théefe to come: And at the time appointed hée
bringeth him thither, for he that could moue him to steale,
could also by secrete suggestion mooue him to goe thither.
The deuill told that the witch should come home with spéed
that had bewitched the butchers son: He that had power in
her heart to make her become a witch, did know he should
haue power to make her with haste to come home. One carieth somewhat which a sick person hath lien in to the cunning man. He can tell, it séemeth, by the smell of the cloth,
whether the deuil hath bene in it (if it smell like his deuill)
and so telleth, the partie is bewitched. Take the clothes
which the sicke partie hath lien in, and burne them, if they
burne blacke, then may you sée it is so, and the witch shall
come in while they be a burning. Nowe, if the Lord gaue
him power, and he hath striken and tormented the bodie of
the sicke person: and if hee haue collourably stirred vp a
witch to send him: Is it not an easie matter for him to
make the fire burne blacke, and to mooue the witch to
come at that present? Or if he haue power for to torment,
and hath no witch to sende him, his great desire being to
haue men guiltie of innocent blood, is it not as easie by the
permission of God, which in his iust iudgment, giueth him
power to seduce such people as will hearken vnto deuils,
for him to make the fire burne blacke, or at least to séeme so
to them, and to mooue some frowarde suspected woman
or other to come in, though she be no witch? A thousande
such things hee worketh in, and as a cunning iuggler can
compasse and bring them about.

    M. B. Indéed an innocent person may come in at such
a time: but I haue heard, I cannot tell howe true it is, that
therefore there is a further thing which they obserue. And
that is this, the cunning man biddeth, set on a posnet or
some pan with naples, and séeth them, and the witch shal
come in while they be in séething, and within a fewe dayes
after, her face will be all bescratched with the nailes. And

I haue heard that some olde woman comming in, her face hath indeed bene as it were scratched within a few dayes after, for the shingles or such like brake forth.

Dan. O the depth of Satans illusions to make blinde people becom witches, and to deale by him. He doth know the corrupted hunfours in the bodie, which will breake out into the smal pockes, or such like, and if he can procure one to come in which is euen ready to haue them, what a shew doth he make, as if the nails did it?

M. B. This were great subtiltie of Satan.

Dan. Nay, we are not able to imagine the depth of his sleights, neither can we see the secrete force, wherwith he moueth the minds of ignorant people, and so bringeth about his enterprifes. There doth lie the greatest cunning of Satan.

M. B. Indeed it seemeth strange and vncredible that the deuil should so moue the minds of men, and lead them vnto this thing and that thing, and in the meane time they doe not know it, but thinke they goe against the deuil. But now I haue a further doubt. I confesse it is an easie thing for the deuill to tell where a thing is that is lost or stollen, but what power hath he to heale that which is sick or sore? Out of question they be innumerable which receiue helpe by going to the cunning men. You say he helpeth the bodie that he may destroy the soule. Hee helpeth that men may seeke vnto him, and so set him, as it were, in the place of God. Me thinketh it should not be in the power of deuilles for to helpe.

Dan. Indeed that is well mooued, there lieth a great sleight of the deuill in it. You say that innumerable do receiue help by going vnto cunning men. I warrant you not so many as you are perswaded.

M. B. O verie manie. There be a number which doe neuer make it knowne, because it is misliked by some.

Dan. Yea, and there be many which come home again

with

with a flea in their eare, they receiue an answere, as good as a slim flam.

M. B. It may be they come too late, the matter is ouer farre spent, and if they had come sooner, they coulde haue holpen them.

Dan. Yea, a number of such cosoning answers the deuill maketh which satisfie ignozant people, which are reaso beleeue all that he telleth, and to daunce after his pipe. One commeth to him foz his childe, if he know the disease be deadly, he will say it is bewitched', but so farre spent, that there is no help, the childe wil hardlie liue two daies: the father commeth home and findeth his child deade, oz it dieth within two oz thzee dayes after, here the deuill getteth credit. Another is sicke and grieuously tozmented, hee sendeth: Satan doth see (foz he sendeth them) that the disease is euen spent, and that the cause of it begin to fail, and so that the partie in a few dayes will recouer, here he prescribeth one paltrie oz other, they vse it, the man is recouered, and so should haue bene without the deuils medicine, but now Satan hath gotten further credite. Another is sicke and languisheth, his neighbours tell him, he may be bewitched, it is good to send, and then he shal know. He sendeth, the deuill doth not know whether the sicke man can escape and recouer, oz not. He saith, it is like he is bewitched: and teacheth what to doe, if there bee any help at all, but doubteth, and so whether the man liue oz die, Satan saueth his credite whole and sound. And many of these answeres he giueth. Againe, we must note that mans imagination is of great fozce, either to continue a disease, oz to diminish and take away some diseases. And in this also Satan deludeth some, foz his medicine seemeth to do somwhat, when it is but the parties conceit.

M. B. These be sleightes indeede: but mee thinketh you goe farre in the last. I doe not see how a mans conceit can help him.

Dan.

Dan. Imagination is a strong thing to hurt, all men doe finde, and why should it not then be strong also to help, when the parties mind is cleared, by beleeuing fully that he receiueth ease?

M. B. But yet it is hard to shewe that euer anie such cure hath bene wrought.

Dan. It is not hard to shew, for that which men doe, it is presumed the deuill can doe the like. And I haue heard of a mery companion that wrought such a cure. Ther was one in London (as report goeth) which was acquainted with Feats. Now, this Feats had a blacke dogge, whome he called Bomelius. This partie afterward had a conceit that Bomelius was a deuill, and that hee felt him within him. He was in heauinesse, and made his moane to one of his acquaintance, who had a merie head, he tolde him, heé had a friend could remooue Bomelius. Hee bad him prepare a breakfast, and he would bring him. Then this was the cure, he made him be stripped naked and stand by a good fire, and though he were fatte ynough of himselfe, basted him all ouer with butter againſt the fire, and made him weare a sleéke stone next his skin vnder his bellie, and the man had present remedie, and gaue him afterward greate thankes.

M. B. I know men haue many foolish imaginations: but though one imagination may driue out another, which is not the curing of any disease in deéd, but of an imagination: yet it doth not followe, that where there is an apparant griefe, that a mans conceit can helpe to cure it.

Dan. Yes, the conceit doth much, euen where there is an apparant disease. A man feareth hee is bewitched, it troubleth al the powers of his mind, and that distempereth his bodie, maketh great alterations in it, and bringeth sundrie griefes. Now, when his minde is freéd from such imaginations, his bodily griefe which grew from the same is eased. And a multitude of Satans cures are but such.

M. B. Nay, there be also euils which be apparant in the bodie, and bee cured, which come not of anie feare or imagination: how can these be cured by any conceit? There is great reason that such griefes may be cured indeede by quieting the minde, as did growe from the disturbance of the same.

Dan. Yea, and that falleth out sometimes in griefes of the body, which doeth not grow from imagination, but from some other passions. As I can giue you an example, which is written and reported by a very reuerend learned Physitian. The cure was done by a lewde cosening knaue in Germanie. A woman had bleare eies that were watery. The knaue lodging there, promised for certainty that hee would heale them: hee did hang a litle writing about her necke, charging strictlie, that it should not be taken from thence nor read, nor opened, for if any of these were done, she could haue no help at all by it. The woman had such a confidence in the thinge, and was so merry and glad, that she left weeping (for her often weeping and teares had spoiled her eies) and so by little and litle, the moysture stayed, and her eies were whole. It fell out that she lost the writing, whereat she was in such griefe and sorrowe, and weeping, that her eies were sore againe. Another founde the writing, opened it, and read it. It was written in the Germane tongue, to this effect translated into English: The deuill pluck out thine eies, and fill their holes with his dung. Was not this, thinke you, a proper salue for to cure her eies? If this medicine had taken effect, her eies should not haue ben healed, but plucked quite out. We may not think but that Satan hath mo cousening tricks than al men in the world, for men are but his schollers. Againe, where men faile, he can worke somewhat in the affections of the parties mindes. And you shall heare them say, when any charme is vsed, you must beleeue it will helpe, or els it will doe you no good at all. Thus if it were well seene into,

the

the greatest part of your innumerable cures, come to bee mere cosonages.

M. B. Well, let all this be true as you haue saide: Yet there be many thinges wherein the deuilles doe helpe. What say you to the boy which healed within few daies after he had scratched the witch, whereas his sores were most grieuous before, and could not be cured? What say you to that which they doe, when butter will not come, or when drinke will not worke in the fat? What say you to the burning of some liue thing, as hogge or henne, and the harme ceassing? And finallie, what say you to the helping of them where the deuill is, and doth torment their bodies?

Dan. All these are answered in few wordes, that where he hath power to hurt either man or beast, drinke or butter he helpeth only by giuing place, and ceassing to hurt, which as I shewed you before, he doth most willinglie, to bring to passe, that men may seek to him, & become euen verie witches. If a man be vexed & tormented by a deuil, & men seek by fasting & prayer to cast him foorth, euen instantly intreating the Lord, then he goeth out with much a do, and vnwillingly, as ouercome & expelled by the power of God. But when he hurteth, as you say he did the butchers sonne, and they seeke to him, and will followe his prescriptions, as to draw blood of the witch, he goeth out willingly, I meane he ceaseth from hurting the bodie: for he goeth not out indeede, but rather goeth further in, and seateth himselfe deeper in the soule. And so is it in all the rest. How gladlie wil he cease to hurte the hennes, so that to please him, a henne may be burnt aliue: his helping is no more but a ceasing from doing harme, if he had power giuen him to hurt.

Sam. This is a strange thing if it be so. There be thousands in the land deceiued. The woman at R. H. by report hath some weeke fourtie come vnto her, and many of them not of the meaner sort. But I doe but hinder, I pray you go forward.

H

Dan.

Dan. The deuill can deceiue thouſand thouſands , and euen the wiſeſt foʒ this woʒld,when they will not be taught of God, but diſpiſe his doctrine , then are they iuſtly giuen ouer to be diſciples of the deuill.

M. B. If there be ſuch deceit in all theſe things, and that the witches do not kill noʒ hurt,but the deuill craftilie ſæmeth to kill and to hurt when the diſeaſes be naturall and maketh the witch beleeue that hee hath done all at her requeſt.Oʒ where God hath giuen him power, he ſtirreth her vp to ſend him,as if either hee could not, oʒ would not meddle,vnles he had bene ſent.Seeing all lieth vpon Satan,it ſhould ſeeme, there is no reaſon that witthes ſhould be put to death:but the ſcripture doth command they ſhuld be put to death.

Dan. The holy ſcriptures doe command that witches ſhou ld be put to death : therein you ſay right: butif you did take it,that the woʒd of God commaundeth they ſhall not be ſuffered to liue,becauſe they kill men and beaſtes,oʒ becauſe they ſend their ſpirits which poſſeſſe men,and toʒ‑ ment their bodies,you are much deceiued:Foʒ you ſhal neuer finde, of all that haue bene toʒmented and plagued by euill ſpirites, that the holte Ghoſte layeth it vpon witches. The cauſes why they ſhould be put to death are , that they haue familiaritie with deuils , which are the blaſphemous enemies of God : and that they ſeduce the people into er‑ roʒr,to runne after deuils,and deuiliſh pʒactiſes,and that they haue ſuch wicked minds. Although they neuer minde to kill oʒ to hurt any , but to doe them good, as they ima‑ gine, yet if they deale with deuilles they ought to die foʒ it.

M. B. Then you take it,that theſe cunning men and women , vnto whome ſo many runne foʒ helpe, which are thought to do very much good,and no hurt at all, ought to be rooted out,and deſtroyed.Let vs knowe what ſcripture there is foʒ it.

Dan.

Dan. Yea, of all other they ought to die, because they doe the greatest harme. Other witches that haue spirites are thought to doe harm, because the deuil at the appointment of God doth harme, and he beareth in hand hee doeth it at the request of the witch: but these that séeme to doe good, do harme indéed, and that many wayes, as euerie one that light in him, may easily sée. And for the scripture s which shewe that they ought to die, reade first in the 22. chapter of Exodus. ver. 18. and there it is said, Thou shalt not suffer a witch to liue.

M. B. That place we take to be meant of these witches which send their spirits to doe harme: the other be not called witches.

Dan. It is that witch that is there commanded to bée put to death, that is called Mecasshephah: such were they and so called, which before Pharaoh did withstand Moses, and made in shewe rods turned into serpents. So that in one kinde the Lord doeth include all such as worke by the deuill. For there be diuers others sortes named in Deut. 18. and they bee all called an abhomination to the Lorde: and no abhomination is to be suffered to remaine among the Lords people. Also in the same place, when he saith, Let there not be found in thée any such or such, as he there reckoneth them vp: It is not alone to will that none should practize such thinges, but also that they should bee rooted out.

M. B. I must néeds agrée vnto that which the worde of God doth set down. But this is the hardest matter of al, how they shall be conuicted.

Dan. Why doe you take it to bee the hardest matter, how a witch shall be conuicted? how is a théefe or a murtherer conuicted but by proofe? If there be vehement suspition, and the party vpon examination confesse the fact, that is a sufficient proofe. If the partie doe denie, and two or thrée of credite doe testifie vpon their knowledge with a so-

lemne

lemne oath, that he is guiltie of the fact, that is also a sufficient proofe. And touching this, God commanded by Moses, that none should dy, vnlesse the matter were proued
against them by two witnesses at the least. Deutronom.
19. ver. 15.

M. B. I graunt, if the partie do denie, and especially,
if the matter touch life, that there ought by the worde of
God to be due proofe by two witnesses at the least. This
may be for murtherers, this may be for theeues : but for
witches I see not how. They deale so secretely with their
spirits, that very seldome they can be conuinced by flat te-
stimonies of men, as to say directly they haue heard or seen
them send their spirits. And againe, it is a rare thinge to
haue a witch confesse. For it is generallie thought the deuill hath such power ouer them, that he wil not suffer them
to confesse.

Dan. O then I perceiue why you account it the hardest
matter of all to conuict a witch, if both testimony and confession doe fayle: but what would you haue further?

M. B. I haue bene of this opinion, that if there were
any likelihood, and suspition, and common fame, that it
was euen proofe ynough, and the best deede that could be
done for to hang them vp, and so to ridde the countrey of
them

Dan. Then you thought that their spirites were hanged with them, and so the country being rid of the witches
and their spirits, mens bodies and their cattell should bee
safe.

M. B. I had a little more wit than to thinke so : but in
trueth it was but a litle more. For I thought if all the witches were hanged, that then their spirits shoulde not haue
anie to hire them, nor to send them to hurte eyther man or
beaste, but I see mine owne follie, and that onlie God giueth the power vnto the deuils to afflict and trie the godly,
and to vexe, torment, and plague the wicked, and that they
shall

shall do this, though all the witches in the worlo were hanged . I know they neede none to cherish them, or to set them a worke.

Dan. But did you not feare if all suspected should be hanged, then some guiltles persons might be put to death? As you see manie that haue bene executed as witches haue taken it vpon their death that they were innocent.

M. B. I will tel you my thought touching that point, which was this. The witches raise tempestes, and hurte corne and fruites vpon the trees, the witches bring the pestilence among men, and murraine among cattell: the witches send their spirits and make men lame, kill their children and their cattell : their spirits cannot bee taken heede of, nor kept out with doores and wals as theeues and murtherers, but come in when they bee sent, and doe so many harmes: for this cause I thought it a marueilous good worke to put all suspected to death, though some of them were innocent, that so sure worke might be made to haue not one left.

Dan. Did you not thinke it a fearfull thinge to shead innocent blood.

M. B. Yea, but I thought it much better that some should be put to death wrongfully', than to leaue any one witch, which might kill and destroy many.

Dan. Then I perceiue that this was the reason which did perswade you, that it was very good to put all to death that were suspected (although it might fall out that some of them were innocent) to auoyde greater inconuenience, and that is, if some few witches should escape, which might plague and kill many. Better a few should be put wrongfully to death, then many should bee tormented and killed, or lamed by the deuilles. But are you still of that mind?

M. B. No verily. For you haue put me in minde that the wicked spirits receiue their power to plague both men and beasts, only from God. They seeke about, they watch

when

when and where hee will giue them leaue to touch, where
God will trie the faith and patience of the iust by him, as
he did in Job, he sendeth him, if he will be sent by a witch, it
is but vnder a collour, shee giueth him not the power, hee
would touch though she were not. Where God will strike
and plague the wicked by him, he giueth him leaue, it is
not the anger of the witch that bringeth it, but their owne
wickednes, whereby they haue prouoked God to displeasure, and so giue this enemy power ouer them.

Dan. Then so long as these two thinges stand, that
God by Satan will afflict in some sort and trie his children (as you alleage he did Job) and that he will vse him
as his executioner, to plague and torment the wicked, as
he sent an euill spirite to vexe king Saule: so long the
harmes done by wicked spirites shall not cease, although
all the witches and coniurers in the worlde were hanged vp. Looke then to the causes, if wee will remooue the
effects. As if thou feare God, and Satan afflict thee, stand
fast in faith and patience, and waite vpon God for thy deliuerance. If thou endure temptation, thou art blessed, and
shalt be crowned. Iam. 1. ver. 12. If thy sinnes haue prouoked God, and the enemie doth touch thy body or thy goods,
fall downe and humble thy selfe with fasting and prayer,
intreat the Lord to turne away his displeasure: looke not
vpon the witch, lay not the cause where it is not, seeke not
help at the hands of deuils, be not a disciple of witches, to
commit thinges abhominable, by polluting the name of
God, and honouring Satan, nor thirst not after the blood
which is innocent, as it falleth out in many.

M. B. I doe assent vnto al this: and surely it is a great
fault to shead innocent blood.

Dan. We may learne in the holie scriptures, that the
sheading of innocent blood is a verie horrible thing in the
eies of almightie God: and a very grieuous thing it is to
haue a land polluted with innocent blood: and that is one
speciall

special cause why Satan dealeth by witches: for he laboureth to wrappe in many guiltlesse persons vpon suspitions, he suggesteth by his helping witches, that ther be many hurting witches in all townes, and villages, that so hee
may set the multitude in a rage, and to suspect vpon euery
likelihood that he can deuise or make shewe of. And thus
whole Iuries must become guiltie of innocent blood, by
condemning as guiltie, and that vpon their solemne oath,
such as be suspected vpon vaine surmises and imaginations, and illusions, rising from blindnes and infidelitie, and
feare of Satan which is in the ignorant sort.

M. B. If you take it, that this is one craft of Satan,
to bring manie to be guiltie of innocent blood, and euen vpon their oathes, which is horrible, what wold you haue the
iudges and Iuries to doe, when any are arraigned of suspition to be witches?

Dan. What would I haue them doe? I would wish
them to bee most warie and circumspect that they bee not
guilty of innocent blood. And that is, to condemne none
but vpon sure ground, and infallible proofs, because presumptions shall not warrant or excuse them before God if
guiltlesse blood be shead.

M. B. It falleth out sometimes when a theefe is arraigned, or a murtherer, that direct euidence faileth, and
yet such circumstances are brought, as doe euen enforce
the Iurie in their conscience to finde them guiltie: It seemeth that this holdeth chiefly about witches, because their
dealing is close and secrete; and it is also thought that the
deuill hath so great power ouer them, that he will not suffer them to confesse.

Dan. Doubting two reasons to prooue that in conuicting witches, likelihoods and presumptions ought to be of
force more than about theeues or murtherers: The first,
because their dealing is secrete: the other because the deuil
will not let them confesse. Indeede men imagining that

P 4   *witches*

witches do worke strange mischiefes, burne in desire to
haue them hanged, as hoping then to be frée, and then vpon
such perswasions as you mention, they suppose it is a very
good worke to put to death all which are suspected. But
touching theeues and murtherers let men take héede how
they deale vpon presumptions, vnles they be very stron g
for we sée that Iuries sometimes doe condemne such as be
guiltlesse, which is an hard thing, especiallie being vpon
their oath. And in witches aboue all other, the proofe s had
néed to be strong: because there is greater sleight of Satan
to pursue the guiltles vnto death, than in the other. Here
is speciall care and wisdome to be vsed. And so likewise for
their confessing, Satan doth gaine more by their confessi=
on, than by their deniall, and therefore rather bewrayeth
them himselfe, and forceth them to confession, oftener than
vnto deniall.

    M. B. These things are beyond my reach, I cannot
conceiue of them. I pray you open it so as that I may perceiue your meaning, and sée some ground of reason for that
which you shall affirme.

    Dan. Then is it requisite to stande vpon them more
at large. And let vs begin with the latter.

    M. B. If you go first to the latter, then shew some rea-
son or experience that Satan bewrayeth the witches, and
draweth them to confesse, and to disclose themselues, rather
than to conceale and hide their doings. I can tell you this
before hand, that the common opinion is otherwise, which
seemeth to be grounded both vpon reason and experience.

    Dan. I know the common opinion is as you say: But
I do much marueill at it, séeing reason and experience doe
proue the contrary as I will shew. As first, touching reason, you will grant, that the deuils dealing altogether by
sleight and subtilties, doe that which doeth most further
their purposes and desires.

    M. B. That is the verie reason why the deuill would
                      by

by no meanes haue the witches bewrayed, as it is thought
becauſe he would lurke ſecretely to doe miſchiefe.

Dan. Indeed it were a good reaſon to proue that part,
if Satan receiued his power from the witch, or could doe
nothing but by her ſending, or néeded to be harboured by
her, or had no minde to meddle, but as it were hired to ſa-
tiſfie her wrath. But ſeeing al theſe be abſurd, and he vſeth
the witch and coniurer but vnder a colour to bring in further euils, it muſt needs followe, that the diſcloſing is ſit-
ter for his purpoſe, than the keeping ſecrete, for if they
ſhould be kept ſecrete, how ſhould he make men think that
he doth ſo many harmes at the requeſt of the witch? howe
ſhould he drawe ſo many to runne after deuils, to ſeek help
at their handes? how ſhould he procure ſo many to vſe wicked and blaſphemous charms and ſorceries, and in ſo horrible maner to abuſe the bleſſed name of God, and his moſt
ſacred word? Or how ſhould he draw the people into manifold errours, and to thirſt euen in rage after innocent
blood? All theſe and a number ſuch like hee procureth and
furthereth, by diſcloſing witches.

M. B. But how ſhall this reaſon be confirmed by experience: No doubt in ſhew he is loath to haue his Dame
(as ſome ſpeake) diſcloſed.

Dan. You ſay well, that in ſhew he is loath to haue the
witch bewrayed: for indéede it is onely in ſhewe, ſéeing hee
would make her and others alſo beléeue, euen when he doth
bewray her by one means or other, that it is ſore againſt
his liking.

M. B. I pray you make that euident.

Dan. When one féeleth himſelfe plagued any way, and
doeth take it to be by Satan, admit it be ſo: he goeth to a
cunning man, and he ſheweth him in a glaſſe, or in a Chry-
ſtall the ſhape of the witch. Who now bewrayeth her?

M. B. That is the cunning mans ſpirite which bewrayeth her, and not her ſpirit which ſhe dealeth withall.

I   *Dan.*

Dan. You are not sure of that : for it may be the same deuill that she dealeth withall , that resembleth her in the glasse: none can doe it better.

M. B. I doe not thinke that he departeth away from her.

Dan. Yea ,but you must remember that she which dealeth with a spirit,dealeth not with a deuill,but with deuils : for manie doe ioyn together.When one of them departeth and carieth the matter to the cunning man, they do not all depart.But what if it be as you said,that som other spirits do bewray, doe you thinke he doeth it against the liking of the witches spirite ? Is Satan deuided against Satan? Will Satan bewray Satan to his hindrance? Remember what our Sauiour hath taught touching that.

M. B. Then if it be so, doe you not take it a sufficient proofe against a witch,euen for a Iurie to finde guilty vpon their oath,if a cunning man by his spirite doe bewray anie.

Dan. It is the most insufficient proofe that can bee, for although he doe tell true in bewraying many, as their own confessions do witnes:yet he doeth it of an euill purpose, he is a lyer,and the father of lies, he desireth chiefly to accuse the innocent, that he may bring men to bee guilty of innocent blood,to make the people beleeue there be multitudes of witches, to set them a work to learne charmes and sorceries, and chiefly, that they may be brought to seeke vnto him , as the bewrayer euen in pitie , of such bad people. Now,because he craftily bewrayeth some', to get credite, shall mens verdict by oath , euen vnto blood, be grounded vpon his testimony ? If a deuill should come in vnto a Iurie,and say the partie about whome you enquire is a witch, should they beleeue him,or wold they say let him be sworn, and witnesse vpon his oath?If not,why should they beleeue that which he hath spoken to the cunning man?

M. B. Surely I am out of doubt he doth all in craft
vnto

vnto a moſt bad purpoſe, and that no credite ought to bee giuen vnto his teſtimony when it is voluntary. But what ſay you to his teſtimonie, when he is euen charged and forced in the name and power of God to tell the trueth: It ſeemeth then he would conceale, but cannot.

Dan. The coniurer which ſuppoſeth that hee dooth bind by the name and power of God to tell him the trueth, is vtterlie deluded. For he is not bound, but is glad that the moſt glorious name of God is ſo horriblie abuſed, and that hee can drawe men into ſuch a gulfe of all abhomination.

M.B. Nay, I doe not meane the coniurer, but when ſuch as be godlie go about to caſt him foorth by prayer.

Dan. This I take to bee your meaning, a man or a woman is poſſeſſed with a Deuill, put caſe it bee ſo indæde (to diſtinguiſh them from ſo many counterfaits, as haue bene) and men aſſemble together where the poſſeſſed is, and cald vpon God, and then charge Satan in the name of Chriſt to tell how hee came there, and who ſent him.

M.B. I meane ſo indæde. And ſome being poſſeſſed, the deuill being charged to tell who ſent him, he hath confeſſed, that ſuch a man did coniure him in thither, or ſuch a witch did ſend him. Shall not this be of force to conuince?

Dan. When any is poſſeſſed by the fiend, mens compaſſion, their loue and pity are to be ſhewed, euen to helpe what they can in ſuch a diſtreſſe. They ought with all inſtant ſuit to intreat the Lord to ſhew mercy, and to expell him. The doctrin of the holy ſcriptures doth warrant this: but for men to talke and queſtion with him, I ſæ no warrant at all by Gods word, much leſſe to command and adiure him to depart. He is the Lords executioner, he hath ſent him, wee may intreat the Lord to remoue him, but what authority haue we to command him to depart, where God hath ſent him?

M.B. Men haue no authority, I grant, but they com

mand

mand and adiure him in the name and power of the Lord,
for to depart.

Dan. That I take ought not to be, for mark this com=
parison: the Prince is displeased with a subiect for some
disloyaltie: An Officer is sent from the Prince to attach
and imprison him: shall he or any other charge this Officer in the Princes name to let him alone, and not to meddle? Is not their way only to pacifie the Prince, and so the
Prince will command the Officer to cease? Euen so, wher
God sendeth Satan his executioner, the only way is to intreat the Lord to be pacified, for then shall the tormentor
no longer remaine.

M. B. Howe doeth this which you speake agree with
that which we read in the Acts of the Apostles, howe S.
Paule commaunded the deuill to come out of a Mayde at
Philippos?

Dan. The holy Apostles and others in the Primitiue
Church, had an extraordinary power giuen them to caste
foorth deuils, and to heale diseases, and they did execute the
same power by the direction and instinct of the holy Ghost:
We may not draw a patterne from that.

M. B. We see that deuils are sometimes expelled.

Dan. They are when the Lord is intreated, otherwise
they but seeme to be bound by adiuration and expelled. But
how can it be prooued, that the father of lies may be bound,
and forced through charge and adiuration in the name
and power of God to tell the trueth? And what warrant
haue we to learne any trueth from his mouth? As to say
we command thee in the name of God, that thou tel vs who
sent thee. Who sent thee? who sent thee? Mother Joan, Mother Joan, saith he: Also we command thee to tell vs, who
sent thee. L. B. coniured me in hither (saith he) Shal wee
thinke he doeth this euen compelled? Or shall we ground
vpon it for certaintie, that he telleth no lie?

M. B. The deuill in a partie possessed hath said, such a
man

man coniured me in hither. The coniurer hath bene put
to death for it, and hath confessed so much. The deuill in an
other hath said, such a woman sent me; it hath likewise bene
confessed by the woman.

Dan. All this maketh for that which I affirme. The
Lord giueth him power to possesse a man. He vnder a collour will be sent by a coniurer, or by a witch: and the one
thinketh the deuill entreth at her intreaty: the other supposeth he doeth euen bind him thereto, whereas he ruleth both
their mindes, and setteth them a worke. Then doeth hee
willingly bewray them, euen for many subtill purposes:
but chiefly, that he may establish coniurations, witchcrafts
and charmes, that he may be sought vnto, that he may set
the people a worke in their calamities to be troubled about
witches and coniurers, as though they could plague, and
neuer looke to God, and that bewraying some witches and
coniurers, he may winne credite, and be belieued, euen
when he accuseth falslie, that he may bring innocent blood
vpon the land. Let all men take heed how vpon their oath
they giue a verdict, especially touching life, vpon his word
howsoeuer he seeme to be forced thereunto: all is most deepe
craft and subtilty in him.

Sam. I pray you giue me leaue to speake a litle. You
say the deuill willinglie bewrayeth witches and coniurers
and that for many subtill purposes. I haue heard of diuers
things done of late which seeme quite contrarie, and that
he taketh it grieuously when they doe confesse and bewray
matters.

Dan. He will seeme to take it in euill part, but let vs
heare the matters, and you shall see plainely that hee iug-
gleth, and maketh shewe of that which is contrary to his
practise.

Sam. Well, I haue heard very credibly, that a woman
of late, suspected another woman to be a witch, & that she
had hurt her some way. She procured a gentleman to send

for the partie suspected, and charging her in his presence, she left her to the Gentleman, who taking her aside, and walking alone with her, began to admonish and perswade her to renounce the deuill & to forsake such wicked waies: While he was thus perswading, and she denying stiffely that she was any such woman, suddainly there appeared some distance from them, a Weasill or Lobsterre looking euen vpon them. Looke (said the Gentleman) yonder same is thy spirit. Ah maister (said she) that is a vermine, there be many of them euery where. Well, as they went towards it, it was vanished out of sight: by and by it appeared againe, and looked vpon them. Surely (saide the Gentleman) it is thy spirit: but she still denyed, and with that her mouth was drawne awrie. Then hee pressed her further, and she confessed all. She confessed shee had hurt and killed by sending her spirit. The Gentleman being no Iustice, let her goe home, and did minde to open the matter vnto some Iustice: When she was come home, another witch meeteth her, and saith, Ah thou beast, what hast thou done? thou hast bewrayed vs all. What remedy nowe (saide she?) What remedy said the other? send thy spirite & touch him: she sent her spirit, and of a suddain the Gentleman had as it wer a flash of fire about him. He lifted vp his hart to God, and felt no hurt. The spirite returneth, and tolde he could not hurt him because he had faith: what then, said the other witch, hath hee nothing that thou maist touch? he hath a child said the other. Send thy spirit, sayd she, and touch the child: she sent her spirite, the childe was in great paine and died. The witches were hanged and confessed.

Dan. What is the chiefe thing which you alleadge this for?

Sam. To shew how vnwilling the deuill was that the witch should confesse and bewray things. No doubt it shuld seeme, that when the Gentleman was talking with her, hee appeared to call her away, for fear least she should confesse:

and

and when she would not come away, he drew her mouth a-
wry:and when she had confessed,the deuill complayned vnto the other witch,and made her chide her.

Dan. The thing is as clear as may be,that he willinglie betwayed them : and will you imagine the contrarie?
Why did he appeare in a likenesse, but euen to enforce her
for to confesse, both by abashing, and giuing the Gentleman euident notice, especially, when he drew her mouth a-
wrie? And why did he set on the other witch to mooue her
that had confessed to send her spirit, but that he would haue
the matter more open,and bring them both to light.

Sam. What should mooue him to bewray the witches?
what could he gaine by it?

Dan. Nay, what almost doth he not gaine by it? Now
all the country ringes of the matter. As if the witches set
on their spirites to lame and to kill : and that they doe not
meddle,but sent by them. He did knowe what power he had
from God to afflict any : he will deale by witches : he maketh others affraid of them, that so they may accuse them.
He findeth meanes to haue all disclosed. Hee mooueth the
witches to send him against the gentleman : hee knoweth
what he can doe: he returneth and saith there is faith : As
though God did not giue him power sometimes to afflict
the faithfull? Or as if he could touch al that haue no faith?
If he could,the greatest part of the world should be destroi-
ed by him. For they be very few in the world in comparison
which haue the true faith. Then must he be sent to the child
that hath no faith : doeth not the faith of the parents holde
Gods protection ouer their infants as ouer themselues?
Here is Satans craft: either he did know by thinges bree-
ding in the bodie of the child that it would at such time fall
sicke and die : and he would be taken to bee the killer of the
childe, to beare in hand that he hath such power & wil doe
when he is requested. Or els he had power giuen him of
God,and wold bring it about this way. If he did strike the

childe, do you imagine he doeth it at her pleasure? Or doe you thinke he would neuer haue thought of any such thing, but moued by her? Doe not all the armies of deuils goe about continuallie, seeking whom they may deuour? Do they not waite where God wil giue them power to strike? Shall we still be so simple as to thinke that women neede to hire or to intreat them to doe harme? Looke vnto God, for those wicked spirits play all parts in the play, and delude both the witches and others.

Sam. I will tell you another thing which was done of late. A woman being suspected to be a witch, and to haue done some hurt among cattell, was examined, and confessed indeed, that she had a spirite which did abide in a hollow tree, where there was an hole, out of which hee spake vnto her. And euer when she was offended with anie, thee went to that tree, and sent him to kill their cattell. She was perswaded to confesse her fault openly, and to promise that she wold vtterly forsak such vngodly waies: after she had made this open confession, the spirite came vnto her being alone. Ah, said he, thou hast confessed and bewrayed all, I coulde teare it to rend thee in peeces: with that she was affrayde, and wound away, and got her into company. Within some few weeks after, she fel out greatly into anger against one man. Towards the tree she goeth, and before she came at it, Ah, said the spirite, wherefore commest thou? who hath angred thee? Such a man, said the witch. And what wouldest thou haue me doe saide the spirite? He hath (saith she) two horses going yonder, touch them or one of them. Well, I thinke euen that night one of the horses died, and the other was litle better. Indeede they recouered that one againe which was not dead, but in verie euill case. Here mee thinketh it is plaine: he was angry that she had bewrayed all. And yet when she came to the tree he let goe all displeasure and went readily.

Dan. Doe you thinke all is plaine here. Indeede here

is that plaine dealing which deuils doe vse. First, doe you thinke Satan lodgeth in an hollow tree? Is hee become so lazy, and idle: hath he left off to be as a roaring lion, seeking whome he may deuour? hath he put off the bloody and cruell nature of the fiery Dragon, so that he mindeth no harm, but when an angrie woman shall intreat him to goe kill a Cow or a horse? Is he become so doting with age, that men shall espie his craft: yea, be found craftier than he is? Alas may there not be deep subtiltie in these things?

Sam. Doe you thinke there is nothing but subtiltie in these things?

Dan. Doe I think there is nothing but subtiltie? Tel me what you thinke. What other end can there be but subtiltie?

Sam. He may haue this purpose (as I think the deuils studie nothing els) to do harme.

Dan. I doe not denie that: for all his craft tendeth vnto harme. But what harme meane you?

Sam. You see here he killed mens cattel.

Dan. It may be he did: but how know you that?

Sam. You see he went at her request & killed one horse, and almost killed the other.

Dan. I wold be loath to adventure my hand vpon that: For who told you, that he killed the one, and almost killed the other?

Sam. The witch her selfe hath confessed the whole matter.

Dan. Who told the witch so?

Sam. Her spirit told her that he did it at her request.

Dan. He is a credible person, and kind hee was vnto her as it seemeth.

Sam. Nay, but we see all things fell out according as she confessed.

Dan. How doe you meane?

Sam. Why, she confessed her fault, the spirite was angrie

k   grie

grie with her, afterward she fell out with that man, and vpon this his horse died, she confessed she sent the spirit, how
could all things fall out so fit?

Dan. The spirite when she came towardes the trée, as-
ked her, wherfore commest thou? who hath angred thée?

Sam. He did so.

Dan. And doe you imagine that the deuill did lie there
and knew nothing vntill she came and told him?

Sam. Why néeded he to aske her if he did know?

Dan. Because hee is subtill: for hee wrought in her
heart, and kindled her wrath, and procured the falling
out betweene her and that man: he did knowe eyther that
the horses at that time had somwhat in them which would
bring death, or els that the Lord had giuen him power for
to strike them: he moued and wrought in her heart to haue
her come againe to the trée: he séemed to be angrie that she
had cōfessed before, but was not, but sought to haue things
knowne. If he had not knowne that the horse should die,
either by some naturall cause, which woulde then breake
foorth, or by some power giuen to him, he wold not at this
time haue moued her heart to goe to the trée. And if her
wrath had without his suggestion caried her so farre, he
could quickly haue turned her: for great is the efficacie of
Satans working in the hearts of such.

Sam. But I marked one thing which you said before,
as that it might be that God giueth sometimes power to
the Deuill, euen at the sending of the witch.

Dan. I say that God in iustice giueth power vnto
Satan to delude, because men refuse to loue his trueth: but
that maketh not that the deuill obtaineth any power to
hurt because the witch sendeth, but the fault is in men, the
sinnes of the people giue power to the deuill: for God is
offended, and sendeth (as *S.* Paule saith) strong delusi-
on. But haue you any mo examples to prooue that the Deuill is not willing to haue witches bewrayed?

Sam.

Sam. I haue heard of many such like, but you say all is but craft, and that he would haue men thinke hee doeth all harmes that are done.

Dan. The Deuill would haue men beleeue that hee doth all, if he could bring it about: And therefore, it is for his aduantage if he doe hurte, to haue it not kept secrete, but openly to be made knowne.

M. B. what say you then vnto this, a witch is apprehended vpon vehement suspition, and caried before a Iustice: he handleth the matter in such sort that she confesseth, as I heard of one not long since: her confession was to this effect: She had two spirits, one like a Weasill, the other like a Mouse. These, she said, did manie thinges for her. Now, she accused a woman about ten or twelue miles off, whom (it may be) she did not knowe, and yet could name, and not only that, but said, the woman had, as it were, a litle bigge in her mouth, where the spirite did sucke blood.

Dan. It is a most easie thing for the deuill to tell witches, that such a man or such a woman is a witch, and hath this or that secret marke vpon them. And within theise few yeares he hath by witches and cunning men, accused such as were very religious and godly. Men must beware that they proceed not vpõ his testimony: he is not to be medled withall, nor any medling which he vseth, is to be taken in good part, seeing he doth all in deep subtilties.

M. B. I do take it, that the testimony of the deuill ought not of it selfe to haue any force with a Iurie, vnlesse it can be proued by some other firme proofes. But what say you vnto this, a witch is condemned, and telleth at the gallows not onlie what she hath done, but also of whom she first had her spirit. She doth this in repentance, and euen readie to depart out of the worlde. It is to bee presumed that she will not in this case lie, nor accuse falsly: Let it be some woman in another towne, whome she saith, brought her the spirite. This woman is also suspected by some of

K 2   her

her neighbours, apprehended and brought to iudgement, and stiflie denieth that she is any witch, or that she euer deliuered any spirite vnto the other which accused her. Nowe here is the question, Is not the testimonie of the woman vpon her death, a sufficient warrant for a Iurie to find this woman guiltie : here they haue now the testimonie not of the Deuill to proceed by, but of a woman, and though not vpon her oath, yet vpon her death, which is no lesse.

Dan. This testimonie may seeme to be sufficient euen to warrant a Iurie to finde guilty, though it touch life : but if we look well into it, we shall see it is not.

M. B. It may be you take it to be infirme, because it is the testimony but of one.

Dan. Nay, not only in respect that it is the testimony but of one, but that it is the testimony of such a one.

M. B. I put the case of such an one as doeth shew repentance, who though she hath bene bad, yet now may bee beleeued.

Dan. I do not meane in that respect, as to say she was a witch, and therefore not to be credited : but if shee repent neuer so much, yet her testimony in this is weake, because she may be vtterly deceiued, and think she telleth the truth, when it was nothing so, but she vtterly deluded.

M. B. Doe you meane, that he may make the other woman thinke, that such a woman deliuered her the spirit, and neuer no such matter?

Dan. Yea, that is my meaning.

M. B. It is farre beyond my reach to see how that can bee.

Dan. You must consider that the deuil doth many waies delude witches, and make them beleeue things which are nothing so. In Germany and other countries, the deuilles haue so deluded the witches, as to make them beleue that they raise tempests of lightenings and thunders. For the deuils do know when these things be comming, tempests of winds, and thunders, and faine would he make the blind world beléeue that those great works of God, be not Gods but his : And that is the cause why he coueteth to appeare in them. These deuils make the witches beléue, that at their request they kil both men and beasts, and many waies afflict, when as many of the things fal out naturally, which they would séeme to doe, and the rest in which they haue power giuen to worke, they stirre vp the witch but vnder a collour for to send them. These deuils make the witches in some places beléue, that they are turned into the likenesse of wolues, that they rend and teare shéepe, that they méet together & banquet, that sometimes they flie or ride in the ayre, which thinges indéed are nothing so, but they strongly delude the fantasies of the witches. Euen so the deuill can delude a poore woman with the likenesse of another woman deliuering a mouse or a catte vnto her, by appearing in such a likenes. Or he can set a strong fantasie in the mind that is oppressed with melancholie, that such or such a matter was, which indéed was neuer so. Men must be wise in these causes, or els may they soon be circumuented by the craftes of Satan and drawen into great sinne.

M. B. If it be thus, then how should a Iurie condemne by their verdict any witch? For she hath not killed, nor the deuill at her request, but maketh her beléue he did it at her request.

'Dan. A witch by the word of God ought to die the death not because she killeth men, for that she cannot (vnlesse it be those witches which kill by poyson, which eyther they receiue from the deuill, or he teacheth them to make) but because she dealeth with deuils. And so if a Iurie doe finde proofe that she hath dealt with deuils, they may and ought to find them guiltie of witchcraft.

M. B. If they find them guilty to haue dealt with deuils, and cannot say they haue murdered men, the law doth not put them to death.

Dan. It wer to be wished, that the law were moze perfect in that respect, euen to cut off all such abhominations. These cunning men and women which deale with spirites and charmes seeming to doe good, and dzaw the people into manifold impieties, with all other which haue familiarity with deuils, oz vse coniurations, ought to bee rooted out, that others might see and feare.

M. B. You will not haue the testimony of Deuils to be of any credit with a Iury, what say you then vnto men, there be some which die, and take it vpon their death, that they are bewitched, and will say pzecisely such oz such haue done it. Foz that is in the other point touching likelihoods.

Dan. They are bewitched indeed, foz the deuill doeth delude their minds: foz you shall finde them able to render no reason but onlie this, in their conscience the partie is naught and they are out of doubt it is so.

M. B. That may bee as you say in some, but I haue knowne a woman my selfe which many haue counted to be a witch, and many things haue fallen out where she hath taken displeasure. Do you not thinke that is a firm pzoofe? She denieth, but the things which fall out, doe manifest her to be naught.

Dan. You must shew the things, and thereby it will appeare.

M. B. She fell out, oz els at the least seemed to be displeased with one, and he had an hogge died suddainlie. An other thought she was displeased with him, and his hozse fell sicke. A third could not sit vpon his stoole at wozke. And within nine oz ten yeares space diuers others. One saw the deuill bigger than a cat with great eies. An other was haunted with a spirite. An other bzewing, the dzinke would not wozke in the fatte. An other sawe a thing in her house as big as a lambe, playing in the window: Another in her grieuous tozment saw the woman stand by her all the night, whom she suspected to bewitch her, and diuers

such

such like, which were too long to recken vp. If she were not a witch, how should all these fall out so fit?

Dan. I haue shewed already, that where Satan hath a witch to deale by, hee bringeth it about, that in all such things as he hath power giuen him of God, he will seeme to do nothing but requested and sent by the witch. In those things which fall out in sicknesses, lamenes & death, vpon naturall causes, he worketh in such sort, as that he maketh the witch beleeue she doeth them. And this hee coueteth to haue breake forth by her confession. Now, where he hath no witch to deale by, he gaineth exceedingly, if hee can worke in the minds of any a strong suspition of any man or woman. For if it be once begun, hee pursueth it with all his power and cunning. If one bee visited with grieuous torment of sicknes, and be so ignorant, and voide of the faith in Gods prouidence, that he imagine the deuill doeth it at the sending by a witch, the deuill will delude him, and make him beleeue that the witch standeth by him. The man or woman suspected cannot come there: Who then worketh that illusion but Satan? Another is affrayde of the deuill to be sent vnto him, by that partie whome he suspecteth to be a witch: and thus through want of faith in God, giueth the deuill the more power ouer him, either to hurt, or to appeare vnto him. For Satan haunteth all men continuallie, seeking all occasions, and needeth not to be sent by man or woman. They be exceeding blind which will reason thus, an euill spirit came and appeared vnto me, after I had angred such a woman, therfore she sent him. Satan if he haue power to doe harme, or knowe where somewhat will follow, is hee not cunning to make the party which shall receiue the harme, to fall out with some that hee may suspect, and so the harme may seem to come from that partie? Againe, in feare, in the darke men take some litle cat or dog to be an vglie deuill. As not long since a rugged water Spaniell hauing a chaine, came to a mans doore

that

that had a saut Bytch, and some espied him in the darke, and said it was a thing as big as a colt, and had eyes as great as saucers. Hereupon some came to charge him, and did charge him in the name of the Father, the Sonne and the holy Ghost, to tell what he was. The dogge at the last told them, for he spake in his language, & said, bowgh, and thereby they did know what he was. If he do knowe where harmes do follow vpon naturall causes in men or beasts, he laboureth either to make them offended, and to fall out with the partie that is suspected, or at the least to perswade the of such displeasure conceiued, that the harms may séeme to come from the same. If he do torment indéed hauing power to possesse the bodie, he will not sticke to lie, and to say such a woman sent him.

M. B. And doeth it not fall out sometimes, that as he saith such a woman sent him, so the woman vpon examination confesseth so much.

Dan. Yea, but I speak where he hath no witch to deale by, but pursueth the innocent with suspition vpon suspition, that men may be guilty of innocent blood. Hee telleth the trueth sometimes, to the end hee may be credited when he doth lie. For let no man be so simple as to thinke, that he will euer tell trueth but for some wicked purpose.

M. B. Yet this of all the rest séemeth most strange vnto me, how so many things should fall out, as it séemeth, after the displeasure of a suspected person, and some of them such as apparantly are done by Satan, as in drinke not working, or in creame, when butter will not come, and yet the party suspected is not a witch.

Dan. Oh sir the sleights of Satan in compassing such matters he marueilous. I knowe it is taken (as they say) to be dead sure that the party is a witch, if sundry such shewes of matters do concurre. But how easie a thing is it for crafty deuils to compasse such matters?

M. B. Then you doe not thinke that common fame
is

is ſufficient to warrant the conſcience of the Iuror, to condemne any.

Dan. Experience doeth teach howe heady much people are in iudging men or women to be witches vpon euerie ſurmiſe. And the power imagined to bee in witches, which breedeth a feare in many, cauſeth them to bee credulous. Many go ſo farre, that if they can intice children to accuſe their parents, they thinke it a good worke.

M.B. You ſay the teſtimony of the deuill is not to bee taken, although it be manifeſt that he doth many times tell the trueth, becauſe when he ſpeaketh the trueth, hee doeth it of a bad purpoſe. And you hold it the teſtimony of the deuil, not only which he ſpeaketh when anie charge him, but alſo which the cunning men & women giue, in as much as they can ſay nothing but vpon his word. Moreouer, vnles I miſtake you, the teſtimony of a witch in many things at her death, is not as you ſay any other than the teſtimonie of the deuil, becauſe the deuill hath deceiued her, and made her beleeue things which were nothing ſo. Beſides al this, you wil haue likelihoods and ſuſpitions to be of no waight, nor common fame and opinion to moue the conſcience of a Iurie, becauſe Satan is exceeding ſubtill in all theſe. Then how ſhall a Iurie finde a witch? What proofes will you haue?

Dan. Men are vpon their oath to deale, & it doth touch life, if they doe finde any guiltie of witchcraft. This is a moſt waightie matter: whereupon it followeth, that there muſt be eyther due proofe by ſufficient witneſſes, or els the confeſſion of the witch. For if the teſtimony be ſuch as may be falſe, as al that commeth from deuils is to be ſuſpected: or if it be but vpon rumors, and likelihoods, in which there may be exceeding ſleights of Satan, as for the moſt parte there be: how can that Iury anſwere before God, which vpon their oath are not ſure, but that ſo proceeding they may condemne the innocent, as often it commeth to paſſe.

L   M. B.

M.B. You mistake one point, for the finding of a witch guilty by a Jury doeth not in all causes touch blood.

Dan. I am not deceiued, for where the Iurie hauing but likelihoods doth find a man or a woman guilty but for killing a beast, it casteth them into prison, setteth them vpon the pillorie, and not only diffameth them for euer, but also if suspition follow again and arraignment, it is death: you sée then how néere a way they haue made vnto blood. But if it touch not blood, but the party escape with the imprisonment and pillory, & neuer againe fall into suspition, how grieuous an infamie is it, to haue bene condemned by Jury to be a witch? I speake it where it is only vpon suspition, or such testimonie as is onelie from Satan, and the partie may be cléere.

M.B. It falleth out sometimes that vpon suspition and common fame they hitte right, and the partie which would not confesse any witchery vpon examination, and arraignment, being condemned doth confesse it.

Dan. Let it be graunted that the Jury vpon Satans testimony, or suspitions and common fame, sometimes hitteth right, which yet I feare is very seldome, that is no warrant before God for men that are sworne, for are they sworne to indict vpō likelihoods, or vpon knowledge in that which vpon sound testimony or confession they shall finde? If the party be a witch which is suspected, & yet no proofe, the Iury doeth more rightly in acquitting, than in condemning, for what warrant haue they vpon their oath to goe by gesse, or to find that which they knowe not?

M.B. I doe take it men offend grieuously, if vpon vnsufficient proofe they condemne the innocent, and especially, because they are solemnly sworne: but if they hit right, though it be only by coniectures and likelihoods, I cannot sée how they should therein offend: they condemne not the innocent, they do the party no wrong.

Dan. I do not say they are to bee charged with any inno-

nocent blood, oz wrong to the partie: but I aske what warrant they haue befoze God vpon oath to touch blood by sufpitons. Admit one be arraigned vpon felony, the likelihoods ar great that he is guiltie of the same, but yet it may
be hæ is clære. What is a Iurie nowe to doe? Are they to
venture vpon the life of a man by their oath by suspitions?
Let it be he is one that God knoweth to be guiltie, but no
man can disclose the same, and therefoze they cleare him,
doe they commit anie offence? Are they bound to find that
which they cannot know? What innocent person then may
not be condemned?

    Sam. I pray you giue me leaue a litle. I doe not well
conceiue this matter about finding out and condemning of
witches. It is somewhat strange vnto me which you speak
I haue my selfe sundry times bene of the Iurie when witches haue bene arraigned, we haue found them guilty vpon common fame, vpon likelihoods, and vpon such testimonie as you disalow. They haue indæd taken it vpon their
deaths that they were innocent, but that neuer made me to
doubt but that they were witches: foz it is saide, the deuill
hath such power ouer them, that he will not suffer them to
confesse.

    Dan. What should mooue you to thinke that the deuill
will not haue them to confesse? you sé some doe confesse
when they be examined, and when they be executed: The
deuil hath power ouer the most desperat thæues aud murtherers?

    Sam. Yea but he careth not so much though the thæues
and the murtherers do confesse, it maketh not so much against him, as when witches bewray all.

    Dan. What, doe you take it he is loath to be diffamed
oz hardly thought off? Otherwise what should it make against him when witches confesse? It is some step to repentance when thæues and murtherers acknowledge
their sinnes, and if he can hinder them, oz hold them des

perate from confessing he will. It is apparant that he coueteth to haue witches to confesse, it maketh so much for
him. He would haue men iudge that there be an hundred
folde more witches than there be. He discloseth by his cunning men & women, and otherwise. He coueteth greatly to
haue it thought that he doeth all, in tempestes, in strange
plagues and diseases which light vpon man or beast. And
for this cause hee maketh the witch beleeue and confesse
more than all, that is, that at her request he did that which
he neuer did nor could doe: vnlesse we will denie the soue-
raintie, and prouidence of God ouer all.

Sam. If Satan gaine so much by disclosing them, what
should be the reason that men are generally perswaded, that
he coueteth to haue the thinges kept secret, and so will not
let the witch confesse.

Dan. It ariseth from false perswasions, and frō a false
feare that witches doe so many harmes, and that at their
sending and request the spirites worke all. If Satan be so
kind and seruiceable to the witch: how is it that he doth not
fetch her some money? For he knoweth where it is lost, or
where it lyeth in mens houses. He telleth the witch he can
make a man lame. He saith he can kill an horse. Yea at
sometime he will say he can and will (if she will haue it so)
kill a man. As if it were in his power to doe many great
thinges, and will not but requested. Let vs see if all the deuils can fetch one peny out of a mans house, whose horse or
cow they say they haue killed. The coniurer, sayth he, can
coniure him into a man, or out of a man: let him coniure
him but into a mans chest if he can, to fetch somewhat from
thence. If the deuils can not do these thinges, then be assu-
red that either they make but a shew of killing and laming,
as they do in the most of such harmes, or else where they do
hurt, it is vpon speciall leaue from God, and not from the
witches pleasure. And to what purpose then should all such
iugglings and shewes serue, if they should be kept close and

not

not confessed.

Sam. Yet for my better satiffaction giue me leaue without offence to lay open some particulars which I haue séen. I was of a Iurie not many yeares paff, when there was an old woman arrained for a witch. There came in eight or ten which gaue euidence againff her. I doe not remember euery particular: but the chiefe for some thinges were of small value. One woman came in and teffified vppon her oath that her hufband vpon his death bed, tooke it vpon his death, that he was bewitched, for he pined a long time. And he sayde further, he was sure that woman had bewitched him. He tooke her to be naught, and thought she was angry with him, because she would haue borrowed fiue shillinges of him, and he denyed to lend it her. The woman tooke her oath also, that she thought in her conscience that the old woman was a witch, and that she killed her hufband. There came in a man that halted, he tolde a shrewde tale. I once, sayd he, had both my legges sound. This old woman and I fell out and did chide. She sayd she would be euen with me. Withn thrée daies after I had such a paine in my knée that I could not ffand. And euer since I go haulting of it, and now and then féele some paine. There came in an other, a little fellowe that was very earneff, me thinkes I sée him yet. He tooke his oath directly that she was a witch: I did once anger her sayde he, but I did repent me: for I looked somewhat would follow. And the next night, I saw the vglieff sight that euer I saw: I awaked suddainely out of my sléepe, and there was me thought a great face, as bigge as they vse to set vp in the figne of the Saracens-head, looked full in my face. I was scarce mine owne man two dayes after. An other came in, a woman and her child dyed with grǽuous paine, & she tooke her oath, that in her conscience she killed her child. Then followed a man, and he sayde he could not tell, but he thought she was once angry with him because she came to begge a few pot-hearbes, and he denyed

her

her: and presently after he heard a thing as he thought to whisper in his eare, thou shalt be bewitched. The next day he had such a paine in his back, that he could not sit vpright: he sayd he sent to a cunning woman, shee tolde he was bewitched, and by a woman that came for pot-hearbes. But she sayd he should recouer of it, and so he sayd he did within some tenne dayes. Then came in two or three graue honest men, which testifies that she was by common fame accounted a witch. We found her giltie, for what could we doe lesse, she was condemned and executed: and vpon the ladder she made her prayer, and toke it vpon her death shee was innocent and free from all such dealings. Do you thinke we did not well?

    Dan. Nay what thinke you? Are you sure she was a witch? May it not be she was innocent, and you vpon your oathes shed innocent bloud?

    Sam. If she were innocent what could we do lesse? we went according to the euidence of such as were sworne, they swore that they in their conscience toke her to bee a witch, and that she did those thinges.

    Dan. If other take their oath that in their conscience they thinke so, is that sufficient to warrant men vpon mine oath to say it is so?

    Sam: Nay, but you see what matters they brought, which perswaded them to thinke so.

    Dan. Might not both you and they be deceiued in your thinking, or may you vpon matters which may induce you to thinke so, present vppon your oath that you knowe it is so?

    Sam. If witnesses come in and sweare falsely, the Iurie proceeding according, their testimonie is cleare from blame, for they goe but by testimonie of men sworne.

    Dan. If witnesses doe sweare directly that in their knowledge a matter was so or so, and sweare falsely, the Iurie is cleare which proceedeth according to their euidence:
vnlesse

vnlesse the Iurie do perceiue that their oath can not be true. But what is that to make the testimonie sufficient where men doe but thinke, and can shewe no necessarie reason to ground their thought vpon? As let vs sée in all these which one could prooue that she must néedes be a witch. One saith her husband tooke it vpon his death that she killed him, because he would not lend her fiue shillings: doth this prooue she bewitched him? Can the deuill kill a man at his pleasure, to gratifie the witch? Is it not rather to be iudged he dyed of some pining sicknesse growing from an euill constitution of body, which the deuill did know, and would set him at some variance with one old woman or other, that so it might bréede suspition of witchcraft.

Sam. You sée there were some things which could not be done but by the deuill.

Dan. In déede the great face which the man thought he saw, was the illusion of the deuill. But is this a good proofe, the deuill appeareth to a man after he hath displeased a woman, therefore she sent him? Doth not Satan haunt all men continually, and would if he could get leaue from God, terrifie them with such illusions? When men are affraide, and haue strong imaginations. What reason did the woman shew which tooke it vpon her conscience that the olde woman killed her child, to prooue that it was so? If shée thought so in her conscience, and tenne thousand more with her vpon bare imagination, was that a warrant for you to sweare solemnely that it was so? As for the testimony of the cunning woman that he was bewitched which had the paine in his backe, vpon the deniall of pot-hearbes, it was the testimony but of the deuill, as I shewed before. And what is common fame grounded vpon imaginations?

Sam. Then you thinke we did amisse do you?

Dan. I would not vpon mine oath doe such a thing for to gaine a kingdome.

Sam. It may be she was a witch, although she tooke it

vpon

vpon her death that she was not.

Dan. It is rather to be thought she was not a witch: for what should make her deny it vpon her death? The deuill had accused her to be a witch, for direct testimonie against her but his.

Sam. You say it was the deuill that told by the cunning woman that she was a witch.

Dan. And do you thinke it was any other but Satan?

Sam. I did not at that time thinke it was the deuill: but now I see it could be none other.

Dan. Then be wiser hereafter, and sorie for that which you haue done.

Sam. In déede I haue cause to be gréeued if shee were not a witch.

Dan. If she were a witch your warrant was small: but she being no witch, you haue taken away both her life, and couered her with infamie.

Sam. I was of an other Iurie since, and there was a woman indicted for a witch, but not for killing any man or child. There came in fiue or sire against her: the first was an old woman, and she sayd she had displeased her, as shee thought, and within two or thrée nights after as she sate by her fire, there was a thing like a toad, or like some little crabbe fish which did créepe vpon the harth, she tooke a beasome & swept it away, and suddainly her bodie was griped. An other fell out with her as she sayd, and her hennes began to die vp, vntil she burnt one henne aliue. A third man came in, and he sayd she was once angry with him, he had a dun cow which was tyed vp in a house, for it was in winter, he feared that some euill would follow, and for his life he could not come in where she was, but he must néedes take vp her taple and kisse vnder it. Two or thrée other came in & sayd she was by common fame accounted a Witch. We found her giltie, and she was condemned to prison, and to the pillorie, but stoode stiffe in it that she was no witch.

Dan.

Dan. And are you ſure ſhe was one?

Sam. I thinke verily ſhee was one, although there be many of her neighbors which thinke ſhe is none: for how could thoſe thinges followe ſo vpon her anger? It ſeemeth they were all done by the deuill.

Dan. He is cunning that can tell that: let it be that it was the deuil which appeared to the old woman like a toad, or like a crabbe fiſh, and that he did gripe her bodie: doth it follow therefore of neceſſitie that the other woman ſent him? He can not turne him ſelfe into any likeneſſe vnleſſe God giue him leaue, as he doth in iuſtice permit that ſo he may delude ignorāt perſons. No witch can giue him power to appeare vnto any in a viſible ſhape. He had this graunted him from God, and Satan by and by will ſet anger, and then appeare, that it might ſeeme it grew from that.

Sam. Wee ſee he appeareth vnto witches, and conturers.

Dan. Yea but we may not thinke he can at his pleaſure take a likenes for to appeare in. That he doth appeare vnto witches and conſurers, it is graunted in Gods wrath to the ende he may ſtrongly delude ſuch wicked people as will not heare and obey the voyce of the Lord God. For the deuils are chained vp by Gods moſt mightie power & prouidence, and in all thinges ſo farre as he letteth forth their chaine, ſo farre they proceede, one inch further they can not proceede. Where men loue darkenes more then light, hee hath leaue giuen him to do many thinges. Some he terrifieth with vgley ſhapes, ſome he intiſeth with faire ſhewes, others he playeth withall in liknes of a Weaſell, or Mouſe, or ſome ſuch ſmall vermine.

Sam. I thought Satan could appeare in what likeneſſe he would, and to whom he would, if the witch ſent him.

Dan. Therein you were much deceiued: for the ſending by the witch can giue him no power, and if he had power, he would no doubt in all places appeare vnto many as farre

and in such sort , as should best serue his turne. Therefore
if he appeare vnto any man, let him thinke God hath giuen
him leaue to goe thus farre with me , and let him call for
faith to resist him, and for true wisedome that he may not
be deceiued nor deluded by him.

Sam. But doth he not appeare sometimes when the
witches send him?

Dan. Where he findeth it is graunted vnto him for to
appeare, he moueth witches to sende him if he haue any to
deale by : but if there be none, yet will he appeare, & deale
so farre as he hath power giuen him.

Sam. But what say you to the womans hennes?

Dan. What should one say to them when they be dead.

Sam. I meane doe you not thinke they were bewitched?

Dan. Christ saith, a Sparrow can not fall without the
will of your heauenly Father : and is not a henne as good
as a Sparrow?

Sam. Nay I am fully perswaded by that which you
haue sayd, that the deuill can not touch any thing to kill or
to hurt it, but vpon speciall leaue from God. They can giue
him no power, she thinketh she setteth him on, and it is he
that setteth her on worke. Let these things be no more called into question : but was it not euident that the deuill killed those hennes? because after the burning of one henne,
the woman had no mo that dyed. If Satan did it not, how
could they cease dying for that? You sayd that he where hee
hath power to hurt in such bodely harmes, is willing to
cease, that such wickednesse may be practised. And then if
this hurt were done by the deuill, is it not to bee thought
that the woman was a witch, seeing it followed after shee
was angry? Let it be that Satan hauing power to do that
he did, would be sent by the witch for a colour, and to make
it euident did set anger betwéen her and that other woman,
to make men thinke that he would not deale , but intreated

by

by her being angry. And so we could doe no lesse but shide
her a witch.

Dan. These be weake foundations to set such a weigh-
tie building vpon. For first it is not certaine that the deuill
killed those hennes. Might it be they had some infection
which he did knowe would kill them, and he craftily bringeth the matter about, maketh two women fall out (which
is the easiest matter of an hundreth) euen vpon the dying of
the hennes, that so it might seeme they were bewitched.
But you say then, how could it be that vpon the burning
of an henne, there dyed no moe, if the deuill did not kill
them? Nay how can you tell but that there should no moe
haue died, although the liue henne had not beene burned?
What if he sawe there should no moe die, and thereupon
moued the heart of that woman to vse that witchcraft in
burning a henne, that it might seeme that was a present remedie to driue away deuils? Or put case he had the power to
kill the womans hennes, eyther he is a weake killer, or else
he goeth to his worke but lazely. He could kill a great heard
of swine quickly when Christ gaue him leaue: could he not
if the woman had fiue thousand hennes, haue killed them all
at once? Why did the foole then but nibble killing now one
and then one, and so was scared away before he had killed
all? If he had power before the henne was burnt for to kill
why did he not then when they went about to burne an hen
kill the rest? It may be he did not knowe what they went
about, he was layd soft in his potte of wooll: and comming
to kill an other henne, he was mette withall, he smelt the
roastmeat, and was scared.

Sam. Then you thinke he did not kill those hennes.

Dan. What certainetie had you that he did kill them?
You found it vpon your oath that he killed them, and that
such a woman sent him and set him a worke, and yet it is
an hundreth to one hee neuer had power for to touch
them.

Sam.

Sam. But what can you say to tye other? The man which could not chuse but kisse vnder his cowes tayle?

Dan. I say he was farre in loue with his cow. Let such men learne to know God, & to expell fantasies out of their mindes that the deuill may not haue such power ouer thē, for he worketh in the fantasies of mans minde, and the more strongly where they feare him, as it appeareth this man did. Satan did worke in this mans minde many foolish imaginations, and to make him beléue he was bewitched he maketh him fall out with one that may be suspected. And thus you Iurie men take your oath & condemne many innocent persons, because you beléue the deuill, & imagine that witches do that which they can not do.

M.B. I haue heard of many that haue béene condemned for witches which haue taken it vpon their death that they were innocent. And sundry of thē haue had farre weaker proofes brought against them then these that haue bin mentioned.

Dan. Yea that is it which I say, men do so little consider the high soueraignety and prouidence of God ouer all things: they ascribe so much to the power of the deuill and and to the anger of witches, and are in such feare of them, that the least shew that can be made by the sleights of Satan deceiueth them. The only way for men that will eschew the snares & subtilties of the deuil and all harmes by him, is this, euen to heare the voyce of God, to be taught of him by his liuely word which is full of pure light to discouer & expell the darke mistes of Satan in which he leadeth men out of the way. and to be armed with faith to resist him, as the holy Apostle S. Peter willeth, so such as doe forsake this way are reduced into grosse errors & into many abominable sinnes, which carrie men to destruction. I must now bidde you farewell.

M. B. I could be content to heare more in these matters, I sée how fondly I haue erred. But séeing you must

be

be gone, I hope we ſhall mæte here againe at ſome other time, God kæpe you.

Sam. I am bound to giue you great thankes. And I pray you when occaſion ſerueth, that you come this way, let vs ſæ you at my houſe.

M. B. I thought there had not bæne ſuch ſubtill practiſes of the deuil, nor ſo great ſinnes as he leadeth mē into.

Sam. It is ſtrange to ſæ how many thouſands are caried away and deceiued, yea many that are very wiſe men.

M. B. The deuill is too craftie for the wiſeſt, vnleſſe they haue the light of Gods word.

The wife of Sam. Huſband yonder commeth the good wife R.

Sam. I would ſhe had come ſooner.

The good wife R. Ho, who is within, by your leaue.

The wife of Sam. I would you had come a litle ſooner, here was one euen now that ſayd you are a witch.

The good wife R. Was there one ſayd I am a witch? you do but ieſt.

The wife of Sam. Nay I promiſe you he was in good earneſt.

The good wife R. I a Witch? I defie him that ſayth it, though he be a Lord. I would all the witches in the land were hanged, and their ſpirits by them.

M. B. Would not you be glad if their ſpirites were hanged vp with them to haue a gowne furred with ſome of their ſkinnes.

The good wife R. Out vpon them, there were furre.

Sam. Wife why diddeſt thou ſay that he ſayd the good wife R. is a witch? he did not ſay ſo.

The wife of Sam. Huſband I did marke his words well ynough, he ſayd ſhe is a witch.

Sam. He doth not know her, and how could he ſay ſhe is a witch?

The wife of Sam. What though he did not know her? did he not ſay ſhe played the witch that hette the ſpitte red

hoat,

A Dialogue concerning

hotte, and thrust it into her creame, when the butter would
not come?

Sam. Indeede wife, thou sayest true, he said that was a
thing taught by the deuill, as also the burning of an henne
or of an hogge aliue, and all such like deuises.

The good wife k. Is that witchcraft? Some scripture man hath tolde you so. Did the deuill teach it? May
the good woman at R. H. taught it my husband: she doeth
more good in one yeare than all these scripture men will
doe so long as they liue.

M. B. Who doe you thinke taught it the cunning woman at R.H.

The good wife R. It is a gift which God hath giuen
her, I thinke the holie spirite of God doth teach her.

M. B. You doe not thinke then that the deuill doeth
teach her?

The good wife R. How should I thinke that the Deuill doeth teach her? Did you euer heare that the deuill did
teach any good thing?

M. B. Doe you know that was a good thing?

The good wife R. Was it not a good thing to driue
the euill spirit out of my creame?

M. B. Do you thinke the deuill was affraid of your spit?

The good wife R. I knowe he was driuen away, and
we haue bene rid of him euer since.

M. B. Can a spit hurt him?

The good wife R. It doth hurt him, or it hurteth the
witch: One of them I am sure: for he commeth no more.
Either she cã get him come no more, because it hurteth him:
or els she will let him come no more, because it hurteth her.

M. B. It is certaine that spirites cannot be hurt but
with spirituall weapons: therefore your spit cannot staie
nor hurt the deuill. And how can it hurt the witch, you did
not thinke she was in your creame, did you?

The good wife R. Some thinke she is there, & therefore, when they thrust in the spitte they say, If thou beest
here

here haue at thine eie.

M. B. If she were in your creame, your butter was not very cleanly.

The good wife R. You are merrily disposed *M.* B. I know you are of my minde, though you put these questions to me. For I am sure none hath counselled more to go to the cunning folke than you.

M. B. I was of your minde, but I am not nowe, for I see how foolish I was. I am sorie that euer I offended so grieuously as to counsaill any for to seeke vnto deuils.

The good wife R. Why, *M.* B. who hath schooled you to day? I am sure you were of another mind no longer agone than yesterday.

The wife of *Sam.* Truely goodwife R. I thinke my husband is turned also: here hath bene one reasoning with them three or foure howers.

The good wife R. Is your husband turned to? I wold you might loose all your hens one after an other, and then I would she would set her spirite vpon your duckes and your geese, and leaue you not one aliue. Will you come to defend witches?

M. B. We do not defend witches.

The good wife R. Yes, yes, there be too many that take their part, I would they might witch some of thē euen into hell, to teach others to defend them. And you M.B. I wold your nagge might hault a little one of these dayes: see whether you would not be glad to seeke helpe.

M. B. I would seeke helpe, I would carry him to the smith to search if he were not pricked or grauelb.

The good wife R. Tush you laugh, If you were plagued as some are, you wold not make so light account of it.

M. B. You thinke the deuill can kill mens cattell, and lame both man and beast at his pleasure: you thinke if the witch intreate him and send him he will go, and if she will not haue him go, he will not meddle. And you thinke when he doth come, you can driue him away with an hoat spitte, oꝛ with burning a liue henne oꝛ a pigge.

The good wife R. Neuer tell me I thinke so, foꝛ you
your selfe haue thought so: and let them say what they can
all the Scripture men in the woꝛld shall neuer perswade
me otherwise.

M.B. I do wonder, not so much at your ignoꝛance as
at this, that I was euen of the same mind that you are and
could not sée mine owne folly.

The good wife R. Folly? how wise you are become of
a suddaine? I know that their spirits lye lurking, foꝛ they
foster them: and when any body hath angred them, then
they call them foꝛth and send them. And looke what they
bid them do, oꝛ hire them to do, that shall be done: as when
she is angry, the spirite will aske her what shall I do? such
a man hath misused me sayth she, go kill his Cow, by and
by he goeth & doth it. Go kill such a womans hens, downe
go they. And some of them are not content to do these lesser
harmes, but they will say, go make such a man lame, kill
him, oꝛ kill his child. Then are they readie and will do a-
ny thing: And I thinke they be happy that can learne to
dꝛiue them away.

M. B. If I should reason with you out of the woꝛde of
God, you should sée that all this is false which you say. The
deuill can not kill noꝛ hurt any thing no not so much as a
pooꝛe henne. If he had power who can escape him? Would
he tarrie to be sent oꝛ intreated by a woman? he is a stirrer
vp vnto all harmes and mischiefes.

The good wife R. What tell you me of Gods woꝛde?
doth not Gods woꝛd say there be witches, and doe not you
thinke God doth suffer bad people? Are you a turnecote?
fare you well, I will talke no longer with you.

M.B. She is wilfull in déede. I will leaue you also.

Sam. I thanke you foꝛ your good companie.

FINIS.

Printed in the United Kingdom
by Lightning Source UK Ltd.
117937UK00001B/397